"This book honors each mourner's journey with empathy, respect, candor and compassion. . . . I found new ideas and approaches on nearly every page."

—Steve Leder, author of *The Beauty of What Remains*

"An incredibly helpful, relatable, and humorous resource for those finding themselves unmoored by the cruel beast that is grief."

—Alyssa Limperis, actress, comedian, and creator of *No Bad Days*

"Finally, a book that makes it okay to grieve messy and makes going through hell just a little bit easier and a lot more fun."

—Katie Rich, writer for *Saturday Night Live* and executive producer of *Chicago Party Aunt*

"In the hardest of times, Rebecca Soffer's warm, reassuring voice is the one I'd want in my ear. . . . She empowers readers to use their own creativity to navigate grief and loss."

—Maggie Smith, author of *Keep Moving: Notes on Loss, Creativity, and Change*

"A soulful, honest, benevolent road map for this trip we all must take, even though we really don't want to. Rebecca is someone you'd want in the passenger seat giving you directions."

—Leslie Gray Streeter, author of *Black Widow*

THE
modern
LOSS

HANDBOOK

AN INTERACTIVE GUIDE
TO MOVING THROUGH GRIEF
AND BUILDING YOUR RESILIENCE

REBECCA SOFFER

RUNNING PRESS
PHILADELPHIA

Running Press
Hachette Book Group
1290 Avenue of the Americas, New York, NY 10104
www.runningpress.com
@Running_Press

Printed in China

First Edition: May 2022

Published by Running Press, an imprint of Perseus Books, LLC, a subsidiary of Hachette Book Group, Inc. The Running Press name and logo is a trademark of the Hachette Book Group.

The Hachette Speakers Bureau provides a wide range of authors for speaking events. To find out more, go to www.hachettespeakersbureau.com or call (866) 376-6591.

The publisher is not responsible for websites (or their content) that are not owned by the publisher.

Print book cover and interior design by Jenna McBride.

Library of Congress Control Number: 2021948246

ISBNs: 978-0-7624-7481-3 (hardcover), 978-0-7624-7479-0 (ebook), 978-1-5491-1074-0 (audio)

RRD-S

10   9   8   7   6   5   4   3

To all the Grief Queens, Kings, and other royalty
who wonder if their stories are worth sharing.
They are.

For Them:

"SEPARATION"

Your absence has gone through me
Like thread through a needle.
Everything I do is stitched with its color.

— W.S. Merwin

- - - - - - - - - - - - - - - - - - -

And For You:

"The most beautiful people we have
known are those who have known
defeat, known suffering, known struggle,
known loss, and have found their way
out of the depths. These persons have
an appreciation, a sensitivity, and an
understanding of life that fills them
with compassion, gentleness, and a
deep loving concern.

BEAUTIFUL PEOPLE DO NOT JUST HAPPEN."

— Dr. Elisabeth Kübler-Ross

Contents

HI, I'M REBECCA, and I wish I had no reason to write this book, just like you wish you had no reason to be holding it, pretty as it may be.

Yet here we are.

So, why am I holed up in a room, overcaffeinated and writing about grief instead of stuff like unlikely animal friendships or the easiest memory-enhancing word problems for humans over forty? Because life.

When I was thirty, my mom, Shelby, was killed in a car accident late one night. She was riding in the family Subaru Outback on the New Jersey Turnpike with my dad, who survived. I'd held her close in a good-bye hug after our annual Adirondack camping trip not even an hour beforehand, assuming we'd be dancing to "September" at my cousin's wedding in Philadelphia the following weekend. Four years later, my dad, Ray, died from a heart attack on a cruise ship in the middle of international waters.

To be perfectly honest, writing this book isn't a project I'd have chosen if someone had presented the possibility to me. My general strategy throughout my twenties had been to build a career in political satire, surround myself with people I loved and who loved me, eat good cheese, and be happy and fulfilled while creating things that made people think, laugh, and feel inspired.

But then my life was cleaved into "The Before" and "The After." For years I was put—and put myself—through the wringer by my grief. I still wanted a career and to create meaningful things. I still wanted to surround myself with people I loved and who loved me. I still wanted to be happy and fulfilled, and to eat good cheese, because to me the former can't exist without the latter. But I found myself mourning a lost imagined future. And without a road map, I didn't know how to do all of that while navigating a life that was accompanied with loss—and one without some of the beloved people I'd relied on to guide me through the world until that point.

My mom was my best friend, and I still miss her and my dad every day. Orphaned at thirty-four was not part of my life plan; I hadn't even thought of the possibility of it happening. But suddenly, I found myself utterly disoriented—confused, horribly sad, sometimes angry, and even jealous of my friends' parents, most of whom were still alive and well.

I felt like I was getting a D-minus in grief simply because I couldn't adequately communicate what I needed to those who cared about me. Just as important, I didn't know how to advocate for myself when people made it clear that they really *didn't* care. I felt like I was failing because I had trouble finding the right professional therapeutic fit. Because I didn't know how to spend my parents' deathiversaries. Because I wasn't adhering to someone else's timeline for how *they* preferred people move through grief. Because I felt so damn alone.

———————— ⌒ ————————

Modern Loss was born in 2013, seven years after my mom died. I cofounded it with my dear friend, fellow writer, neurotic New York City Jewess, and commiserator-in-grief, Gabi Birkner. It exists because we couldn't find anything else that spoke to us with warmth, encouragement, and casual realness about this messy ride. Initially, it was a website publishing candid personal essays and tips. But Modern Loss quickly established itself as a platform for these conversations across all types of media and events.

Our website has published nearly two thousand original personal narratives, advice columns, and practical resource pieces that have been read by millions. We've offered hundreds of community sessions featuring authors, therapists, experts, wellness practitioners, and even some "rage baking" classes (if that phrase doesn't make sense to you, you probably just haven't needed it yet). We've produced live storytelling events around the United States (and during Covid-19, several virtual ones—"The Zooming of Grievances" Festivus celebration, among them) with a fascinating and diverse range of people, all with unique stories about loss—its impact, its aftermath, and the strange and scary new territory a griever must find a way to navigate, or at least try to.

In grief, we are all beginners, and the landscape is changing all the time. Throughout the evolution of Modern Loss, we have stayed true to our tagline: Beginners welcome.

There is no healing without acknowledgment. Difficult emotions don't just go away if you pretend they don't exist (or if some people seem to be asking you to do so, and trust me . . . *they will*). I spent too long trying to feel validated in my grief by those around me—many of them well meaning, sure, but most with no idea how to make me feel seen and heard. I couldn't figure out how to say what I was feeling or identify what might help mitigate that feeling or make it even just a tiny bit less brutal.

What I finally realized was this: As completely unfair as it felt, absorbing my grief, figuring it out, and living with it were my responsibilities. Nobody else could do it for me. It was only when I started to really listen to myself—what I was feeling, what I wanted to share with the world—that I began to feel more firmly planted on the ground, in the world, and in my life. And at that point, I started to become more acutely aware of my resilience.

Modern Loss was founded on the tenet that storytelling is a change agent for both the storytellers and those who hear them. We encourage everyone to get to the point where they are sharing their own narratives with the world instead of letting the world assume it knows what those narratives are. So, what better way to keep track of our own stories than to create a dedicated space to reflect on them as they evolve? What better way to activate curiosity and choose to see the truth in our lives than by creating a container that helps you think about how grief has shaped your life?

That, conveniently, brings me to what you'll find within these pages.

The goal of this handbook is to help you do three things: stay connected to the person who died (henceforth referred to as "your person"), stay connected to the world around you, and, of course, stay connected to yourself.

When you manage to do all of that, you will begin to write your own narrative—one that is unique to you and bends and breaks and shifts but still exists. That acknowledgment creates a baseline of resilience, which simply means to be aware of possibility even while feeling complete devastation.

Life and death are intimately linked; this book will help you weave your grief into your life in a way that is practical, creative, comforting, provoking, a bit fun, and, finally, hopeful.

This is *not* your old-school grief book. You'll find no angels, pastels, or kittens (though I *do* love kittens; please, I'm not a monster). It offers no toxic positivity or suggestions that you find gratitude in everything. Sure, there are things to be grateful for. But this is the place to honor *all the feelings*. So, it's 90 percent grief, 10 percent gratitude and 0 percent platitude. (Actually, there are some platitudes later on, but I'll encourage you to quite literally rip them into pieces.)

Some people may be telling you to "move on" because "it's time." But this handbook is an interactive guide that holds space for your loss. (Refer back to our zero-platitude tolerance.) There's room for journaling, but it's also your task manager, idea catcher, inspiration, friend-you-can-scream-into-the-cosmic-void-to, sketchbook, and memorial.

Everyone, at some point, will experience the loss of a meaningful being. Grief has no standards; it will attach to anyone. As such, there is no possible way this handbook can take on every single facet of grief. Some parts may not apply to you. My hope is to offer an engaging place to grow your thoughts and feelings as they evolve and pop up, a place that will help you create a road map to exercise your agency and feel secure in developing how you want to live with grief. If you find a page you don't feel applies to your experience, tear it out, fold it into a fan or a flower, stick your gum in it. Or just leave it blank for now, because you might be surprised by how it resonates with you later on.

I don't believe in consecutive stage-based grief models, unless you count "utter shitshow" as an official consecutive stage-based grief model. So, there's no set "course" or order in which to do this book. It's meant to be done in any order you like . . . just like the experiences of real grief. Most important, there are no rules and no judgment. At Modern Loss, we always say, "As long as you aren't harming yourself or anyone else, you do you."

Speaking of taking care of yourself, this book is not meant to be a substitute for therapy or other professional medical or mental health support. Some of its sections, prompts, and your responses might even be something you want to share with your provider.

Like the Modern Loss website, community, and my first book (*Modern Loss: Candid Conversation about Grief. Beginners Welcome.*), this handbook is about honoring your unique grief journey and finding points of connection with fellow travelers. Wherever you are, be it still on the on-ramp or miles down the road, you may have already realized that life after loss is full of messiness, melancholy, and macabre hilarity.

What I hope you know—and what I hope this book helps you to remember—is that your relationship with your person isn't over just because they're dead, and your own life has enormous potential for richness.

This whole "life after loss" thing isn't black or white but rather all the shades of gray imaginable. Not everything will be okay. But a lot will. Eventually.

Use this handbook as a private place where you can try things out, confide, think things through, remember, mess up, and try again. Try engaging with it for a few minutes at a time at first. Feel free to throw it across the room, doodle all over it, let your cat sleep on it, or ignore it for months and then come back to it. I certainly won't take it personally.

Remember: Grief isn't an illness. There's no vaccine for it, no "cure." And be wary of anyone who suggests otherwise! Grief is an active, dynamic, living thing—an entity all its own that changes within and alongside you and sometimes even in spite of you. It's the ultimate shape-shifter, appearing as both massive depression and major motivation—and everything in between. It can both muddle our vision and allow us to see clearly. And it can help us live and think and love and connect in ways in which you could never have anticipated or imagined.

Whenever I'd say good-bye to my mom, she'd share the same parting words: "Take care of my girl." In fact, they happened to be her forever parting words on that terrible night. It took me a long time to figure out how to do that, and some days still have me scratching my head as to how. Just like weather, grief changes—sometimes in an instant. But I've learned how to walk through its varied landscapes, even if I'm weeping or stumbling or skipping or even sometimes peacefully strolling along through the weeds and large rocks. And as I've come to learn, and I hope you will, too, using this handbook as a resource: I've got this, even when I think I don't.

So, take care of you. You've got this, even when you think you don't.

Guiding Principle for Using This Book

BEFORE YOU TURN THE PAGE, may I suggest a bit of a mental shift?

When it comes to facing hard things, our culture is obsessed with war metaphors. We just *looooove* to imply that if you care enough or fight hard or long enough, you'll vanquish the aggressor. "You're so strong," people automatically assure someone dealing with a major health issue because they don't know what else to say that sounds motivating. "You'll win this battle."

This is incredibly grating when it comes to framing how someone died—a person who dies from cancer is no less brave than one who doesn't. It's also grating because, when we continue to promote this imagery of a battle cry and military strategy as the ideal way to tackle grief, we end up unwittingly absorbing part of the message. So, when it's our turn, we buy into the myth that we can control things through strength and sheer willpower. And then it hits us that, *wait, I'm forcing myself to push and push, day after day, and I don't feel like I'm winning* anything.

Listen, if you keep on furiously powering through adverse situations, especially ones that will permanently alter your life and need to be viewed as a marathon instead of a sprint, eventually you're gonna power yourself right off a cliff. There's no winning or losing in tough times (over most of which you have only so much control, by the way). There's no war. This isn't freaking Desert Storm. There's just doing. And then waking up and doing again. The pandemic has taught us that in spades.

With that in mind, you know what I think is cooler than a war metaphor? A crab one. (Hear me out.)

First, did you know that the horseshoe crab is the most successful animal on Earth? (And that they aren't actual crustaceans? But just go with it because it fits within the metaphor I'm following.) I won't go into all the fascinating details about how they've lasted 440 million years longer than humans, surviving asteroids, at least three ice ages, and sea level changes. Or how they've developed a number of adaptations that allow them not only to survive but also to thrive, including a primitive immune-like response to bacteria and a specialized assortment of appendages. But it's all pretty cool stuff.

Now consider the sand crab. Their only real job is to grip tightly onto their bearings, which means they spend most of their time buried in shifting sand. They don't fight it. Instead, these teeny tiny creatures bend and shift by using flexible footwork, digging in and letting go as needed in order to maintain their balance. They keep going when they lose a limb (and sometimes even grow it back). They find a way. Always, and no matter what.

Finally, think about all the other crabs out there, from the ones on the beach, to mud crabs, to hermit crabs in a cage. Most move in any direction

as needed—forward, backward, and some even sideways, depending on the situation. They don't try to follow any particular trajectory. They change course when something isn't working for them—and decide pretty quickly when it isn't.

In sum, you can't fuck with a crab. They're resilient. They get shit done. And they don't care if they look wonky while doing it; they just do it.

Grief is different for everyone, even when we're mourning the same person. There are endless permutations and combinations to how our particular personalities weather grief over someone with whom we had a unique relationship. As such, we need to be a little flexible in order to stay "strong."

Remember that strength looks like a lot of things, from "powering through" on some days to giving yourself space to collapse into a crumbled, snotty heap on other days. Remember that bravery can look like completely screwing it up or not getting it quite right and then trying again. And remember that if something isn't resonating with you, you can always pivot and see what works better. Think like a crab.

Grounding Affirmations

FOR SO LONG, I felt completely unmoored in my grief, as though I were free-floating through a once-familiar universe, untethered from everything I'd known beforehand. But the Earth had the audacity to keep spinning, and I had no choice but to find ways to anchor myself when nobody else could anchor me.

Sometimes, though, you don't have time to thoughtfully search for those anchors, like when you start crying in front of the clearance rack at Kohl's or have an anxiety attack when your person's doppelgänger jogs by you in the park. So, I've found it helpful to have a few affirmations to mutter to myself when the going gets tough, confusing, or just downright exhausting. They remind me of who I am, why I'm here, and where I'd like to head next.

A few of my favorites:

> THIS, TOO, SHALL PASS.

> CALGON, TAKE ME AWAY!

> NO FEELING IS FINAL.

The first is courtesy of my maternal grandmom, Sylvia, whom I adored and who lived through some *stuff*. She'd gently assure me that whatever I was experiencing—from mildly stressful to downright terrifying—would indeed pass. And she'd do it while clasping my hand between her soft palms, calling me her *shayna maidel* ("pretty girl" in Yiddish), and insisting I overeat whatever she'd just cooked in her tiny, delicious-smelling Northeast Philly kitchen.

It reminds me that whatever awful moment I'm in is finite in some way and soothes me with the knowledge that I was loved by, and loved, some pretty wonderful people.

The second, because I'm a proud GenXer who vividly remembers the "Calgon, take me away!" commercial despite never having actually used the product. Whenever I whisper that phrase, I'm magically transported to a circular bathtub overflowing with bubbles and encircled by strangely large ionic columns, with hair that is perfectly pinned up and miraculously dry. Also, I giggle a bit because that ad was preposterous.

The third, because it's true. It's a line from Rainer Maria Rilke's poem "Go to the Limits of Your Longing" and just kind of stuck with me. But I seem to always forget it in the heat of the moment. (See the "Accurate Stages of Grief" on page 62 for proof of how frequently those feelings ebb and flow.)

This list is a living thing that will shed, grow, and change just as grief does. One suggestion might feel more helpful on Monday than it does on Thursday, and that's just fine. The most important thing is that no two will ever look exactly alike.

Come up with your own affirmations, and keep a running list below.

_____   _____
_____   _____
_____   _____
_____   _____
_____   _____

What Is Resilience, Anyway?

ri-ˈzil-yən(t)s (noun)

1: the capability of a strained body to recover its size and shape after deformation caused especially by compressive stress

2: an ability to recover from or adjust easily to misfortune or change

I WON'T BLAME YOU for rolling your eyes at the name of this section. After all, "resilience" has become an overused pop psychology buzzword/hashtag in the same vein as "self-care" or "me-time" or "mindfulness."

But resilience is, in fact, something you should learn more about. It's the thing that enables you to experience post-traumatic growth, recognize possibilities, and find new sources of meaning along the long arc of loss. And as someone who is still very much alive, you deserve to have all that.

Those unicorns who've never encountered any major obstacles may not understand how resilient they are. It's only when life tosses those curveballs—death, illness, job loss, devastating breakups, physical traumas, sudden loss of home or access to integral things like education and safety, other failures or disappointments—that our resilience comes through. The good news: We are designed to be resilient. It is our birthright.

You will *not* get any toxic positivity in this book. I'll never say, "Everything happens for a reason," because I don't believe it does. I'll never say, "Everything will be okay," because it won't (though was it ever, really?). But I will encourage you to use your agency, because we humans have an innate capacity to adapt to loss and function healthily. My friend and mentor, Ruth Ann Harnisch, has helped me to understand how the phrase "empower yourself" isn't an entirely accurate goal. Why? We already have the power within ourselves. We just have to use it.

For me, the phrase "it is what it is" reminds me of my power. It suggests that I have no control over what happened in the past and yanks me into the present so that I can figure out what I *can* control and exercise my agency accordingly. And that does create a feeling of being empowered.

Resilience is a critical skill, and many factors contribute to our ability to build it up. But we are all resilient. It's a matter of leveling up when you need to come through for yourself or maybe for someone else. And it can sometimes be seen in light of what you've already endured, whether it's surviving the earliest days of the most profound grief or some other prior life setback that you muddled your way through. Take a minute to consider your own experiences.

Your way of coping with a challenging situation could be completely different from someone else's. Some of us have easier times picking ourselves up than others. But guess what? We aren't born with a set amount of resilience. It's not predetermined, like male pattern baldness or height or whether cilantro tastes like soap. It's a muscle that can be activated and strengthened. On the flip side, it can also be ignored, and then it may become atrophied.

It's never too late to start this work, and even if you don't feel like it, you're certainly already doing at least some of it. Think of this book as full of various-size weights and exercises you can try—with those all-important reps, of course—that will help you to strengthen your resilience muscles. That is truly your superpower. You don't have to earn it; you've just got to tap into it, tend to it, and build it.

Just as it takes time to build noticeable triceps with a Bowflex (or so the infomercials tell me), it takes time to build resilience and noticeable growth from your trauma. It could be a while before you stop yourself and realize that you moved through a big decision, a milestone day, or just a Thursday night without needing to release a primal scream. But it will happen, especially if you give yourself compassion throughout the process. Putting one foot in front of the other adds up.

Remember, you can do hard things.

"It takes enormous trust and courage to allow yourself to remember."

— Bessel Van der Kolk

What Was,
What Might Have Been,
and What May Be

———

ALL MEMORIES, THOUGHTS, AND HOPES WELCOME

Holding Onto Memories Without Being Held Back

YOU'VE PROBABLY HEARD the phrase "Grief is love with nowhere to go." One minute our person is here, and the next they're just . . . gone. But the love, passion, anger, sadness, hopes, and everything else that make a relationship dynamic still exist. As the individual left behind, you evolve, and so does the way in which you relate to your person. The intensity of your grief may equal the depth of your love, confusion, or anger.

Know that the relationship changes but lives on. If you're in the early days of grief, this might be hard—even impossible—to imagine, because those days tend to be wrapped up in memories of illness and death and early loss. You're busy with preparations, signing forms, and dealing with grim or difficult logistics. **But even when someone dies, you are still in a relationship with them, and you will continue to understand and nurture it in new ways as you move through the long arc of loss. Nobody can take away the connection.** If your child died or if you miscarried, you will always be that child's parent. If your partner died, you will always be their partner, even if there are others down the line. If your parents or sibling died, you will always be their child, brother, or sister. If you lose a friend, you will always be their friend.

We can make the conscious choice to reflect on the past, and we absolutely should because the past holds both beautiful memories and bitter learning experiences. These two realities working together can bolster and sustain us, although we likely have to move through some tears first. That's okay.

We can also choose to reflect on our hopes and dreams for the future that will either go unrealized or take a totally different form from what we ever expected. We say people are "gone." But they are extremely alive in our thoughts and memories, and that stuff is *real*. You can have rituals that honor them, change alongside your grief, or remain traditions, and you can have a relationship with them through memory. What you need to ask yourself is how you can personally maintain, sustain, interrogate, and nurture a relationship with your person now that they have died. This requires curiosity and compassion for yourself and for your person.

I've learned so much about this from the Modern Loss community. There's the man who read children's books at his daughter's grave for a full year, or the woman who started an Instagram account to share all the dumb-yet-hilarious memes she'd have ordinarily shared with her dead brother, or the one who went alone on the dream trip she had planned with her husband and brought along his ashes to scatter there.

AVOCADO—
IMMEDIATE; LIKE, WHEN YOU'RE
STILL IN THE STORE HOLDING IT

EGGS—1 MONTH

MAKEUP—2 YEARS

PICKLES—5 YEARS

INSTANT COFFEE—25 YEARS

HARD LIQUOR, DRIED BEANS,
GRIEF, WORCESTERSHIRE SAUCE,
AND HONEY—NEVER

Here are some prompts to help you reflect on what was, what might have been, and what may be. Consider these starting points for reflecting on the past and exploring what your feelings on the future are. While not every prompt will apply to your loss, it might spur other thoughts and reflections.*

What the World Thinks I'm Grieving

My person

What I'm Actually Grieving

My person

The person I used to be before they died

The dynamics with everyone else in my life, which have all shifted in their absence

The milestones my person will never celebrate with me

The conversations I wish we had

The people who've come into—and will come into—my life who they would have loved and who would have loved them

The milestones they will never hit and all the dreams I had for them

Everything else that could have been

*If you run out of space, there are extra notes pages at the back of the book.

What Was

STEPHEN COLBERT:

"WHAT DO YOU THINK HAPPENS WHEN WE DIE, KEANU REEVES?"

—

KEANU REEVES:

"I KNOW THAT THE ONES WHO LOVE US WILL MISS US."

List five to ten qualities you think they embodied: the good, the bad, the quirky, and the ugly.

_____

_____

_____

_____

_____

_____

_____

_____

_____

_____

_____

_____

What did you love most about your person?

_____

_____

_____

_____

_____

What's the one thing that always reminds you of your person?

_____

_____

_____

_____

_____

What annoyed and/or infuriated you about your person? (It's okay, we're all human.)

_____

_____

_____

_____

_____

_____

_____

When you close your eyes, what's the first image of your person that comes up? (This could change from day to day or even from moment to moment.)

_____

_____

_____

_____

_____

Is there any achievement you accomplished together?

_____

_____

_____

_____

_____

When did they seem most proud of you?

_____

_____

_____

_____

_____

_____

What was an extremely private moment you shared or loved sharing repeatedly with your person?

_____

_____

_____

_____

_____

Did they have any life mottos? Favorite sayings? Include the ridiculous stuff as well as the profound. I promise you'll want to share it with someone one day, or at least remember it.

_____

_____

_____

_____

_____

What was their favorite place and why? Where did they want to go but never got to visit?

_____

_____

_____

_____

What songs remind you of them?

_____

_____

_____

_____

_____

What were their favorite movies?

_____

_____

_____

_____

_____

What was unique about your relationship that no one else could make
claim to?

_____

_____

_____

_____

_____

_____

_____

What were some of the things you disagreed on? Did you resolve them?

_____

_____

_____

_____

_____

_____

How did they make you laugh?

_____

_____

_____

_____

_____

How did you make them laugh?

_____

_____

_____

_____

_____

What were their favorite foods?

_____

_____

_____

_____

_____

What did they consider to be their greatest achievement? What do you think it was?

_____

_____

_____

_____

_____

Did they ever embarrass you, or vice versa? Consider even the silly stuff.

_____

_____

_____

_____

_____

_____

_____

What were their most valued possessions?

_____

_____

_____

_____

_____

_____

What scents remind you of them?

_____

_____

_____

_____

_____

_____

What's the biggest risk they took in their life? Did it pay off?

_____

_____

_____

_____

_____

_____

Write down some of your favorite stories involving your person.

_____

_____

_____

_____

_____

_____

_____

_____

_____

_____

_____

_____

_____

_____

_____

_____

_____

_____

_____

RELATIONSHIPS PEOPLE CAN MINIMIZE

- a parent figure
- a colleague
- an honorary relative
- a pet
- a patient, student, mentor
- a fertility dream never to be realized

What Might Have Been

Envision your person beside you right now. What would you talk about?

_____

_____

_____

_____

_____

What have you accomplished or what are you working toward now that you'd want to share with them?

_____

_____

_____

_____

_____

If you could travel back in time or to an alternate future, what would you want to tell them?

_____

_____

_____

Write down all the future milestones you wish you could have experienced with your person and how you envisioned your roles.

_____

_____

_____

_____

_____

_____

Start a letter, or a laundry list, of things you wish you'd said—or would be able to say in the future—to your person. Add to it whenever you like.

_____

_____

_____

_____

_____

_____

_____

_____

_____

_____

_____

_____

_____

What May Be

"Ain't no shame in holding onto grief, as long as you make room for other things, too."

—Bubbles, The Wire

ALTHOUGH IT MAY seem like one more difficult task to complete, there is great benefit in digging deeper into your relationship with grief while also envisioning how you'll evolve as your grief shifts. Even if it sometimes feels like it won't, it will. The only permanent thing is change, and that applies to grief as well. Think of a natural landscape—the weather shifts, the seasons change. Learning to navigate different seasons, through storms or sunlight, through disorientation and clarity, is a skill—a gift, really—that will serve you well.

People talk about "getting over" loss, but that's just not possible. There's no way you'll ever stop thinking about your person entirely. To suggest otherwise is unrealistic and can feel like punishment (and, jeez, can we agree that grief is punishing enough on its own?). The more realistic goal is to integrate the loss into your life: through memory, remembrance, tears, or conscious exercises like the ones below. Shift your mindset. Don't think of grief as a wall to scale but rather as a wall to walk alongside—one you can decorate, too.

What's one thing you wish for your future self as someone living with loss?

_____

_____

_____

_____

_____

Is there anything you changed or might change in your life (career/partnership/focus) as a result of grief?

_____

_____

_____

_____

_____

How do you envision moving through the crucible of grief changing you? (As ever, the good, the bad, the ugly. No judgment here, so be as honest as you can.)

_____

_____

_____

_____

_____

Is there anything your person did that impacted you after their death and that you'd do differently? Did they promise to leave you something and then didn't? Did they not leave specific instructions for their funeral or memorial or something else that resulted in stress and confusion? Map out *everything*, then dog-ear this page and make sure you formalize some of your wishes. Trust me here.

_____

_____

_____

_____

_____

_____

_____

_____

_____

_____

_____

_____

_____

_____

_____

_____

If you didn't feel so burdened by your grief (not that the grief is gone but rather that it isn't holding you back so much), what might your life look like?

Relationships?

_____

_____

_____

Hobbies?

_____

_____

_____

Career?

_____

_____

_____

Nights on the couch?

_____

_____

_____

What activities might you be doing to mark milestones in your person's absence?

_____

_____

_____

_____

_____

_____

_____

_____

What's something you've been feeling guilty about or burdened by that you hope to feel ready to let go of? (This might especially pertain to those who have been living with loss for quite some time.)

_____

_____

_____

_____

_____

_____

_____

_____

The Tough Stuff*

*only do this when you feel ready

"Grief takes many forms, including the absence of grief."

— Alison Bechdel

NOT EVERYTHING in our memory is positive or pleasing. Our relationships aren't limited to joyful school recitals, heartfelt birthday cards, or intimate pillow talk. But what do we do with all the other feelings that aren't as easy to manage, understand, or mitigate?

It's no secret that our connections are complicated, dynamic, and multi-layered. Often that means even in our best relationships and even with those we've lost, there's still the sticky wicket stuff. As my cofounder, Gabi Birkner, would say, we are imperfect humans grieving imperfect humans imperfectly.

We're people. We hurt each other (and ourselves) in seemingly endless ways, sometimes without trying to and, frankly, sometimes intentionally (which leads to regret, another possible, powerful feeling after someone dies). We make mistakes that we never reflect on or apologize for. We never get to say "I love you" again.

And yet society prefers that we put the emphasis of remembrance on the happy, the supposedly perfect, the lightness, instead of the dark under-belly of grief. The stuff you want to push far away but that deserves as much space for examination as the comforting stuff. In fact, I'd argue that it might deserve even more than remembering someone's favorite food.

You don't have to answer questions about why or how someone died unless you want to. You don't owe anyone the details (especially the grief voyeurs you'll meet along the way). But it might help to write down some of the things you're struggling with here, because it's a lot to hold on to.

Please remember that this is enormously beneficial stuff to get out. But this is just a handbook! If you wish to examine whatever comes up more deeply, please consider talking to a therapist who can help you work through it. (Coincidentally, there's a whole section on that on page 68.)

What memories of your person do you wish you could forget?

_____

_____

_____

_____

_____

_____

_____

_____

_____

_____

_____

Do you feel you failed them in any way?

_____

_____

_____

_____

_____

What was their biggest regret?

_____

_____

_____

_____

_____

Are there ways in which you hurt them? If you never got to apologize, use this space to write what you wish you'd said or done instead.

_____

_____

_____

_____

_____

_____

Are there ways in which they hurt you? If they never apologized, what do you wish they would have said?

_____

_____

_____

_____

_____

What did you never understand about them that you're starting to understand now?

_____

_____

_____

_____

_____

Were you ever estranged from your person? What feelings come up around that?

_____

_____

_____

_____

Was your person ill? If so, what sort of emotions does that bring up?

_____

_____

_____

_____

_____

Are there any behaviors your person had that you're angry with them about? Anything that you feel (secretly or outwardly) contributed to their death?

_____

_____

_____

_____

_____

Are there any secrets you discovered after their death that you are struggling with?

_____

_____

_____

_____

_____

Do you feel bad that you survived and they died? What thoughts come up around this?

_____

_____

_____

_____

_____

_____

_____

Do you resent anything about your person or the circumstances of their death?

_____

_____

_____

_____

_____

_____

_____

_____

CRYING IN PUBLIC VERSION!

BINGO

B	I	N	G	O
ON A WALK	AT THE GYM	AT THE PLAYGROUND	AT SCHOOL DROPOFF / PICKUP	ORDERING COFFEE
IN CLASS	AT WORK	ON A FIRST DATE	AT A LIVE PERFORMANCE	ON PUBLIC TRANSPOR-TATION
WITHIN SHRUBBERY IN WHICH YOU UNSUCCESSFULLY HIDE	AT CHURCH / TEMPLE / MOSQUE		IN A THEATER WATCHING A MOVIE STARRING THE ROCK	IN YOUR CAR WHILE STOPPED AT A LIGHT
TO A KIND / SHOCKINGLY UNKIND CUSTOMER SERVICE AGENT	AT A TAMPON COMMERCIAL	AT A DISNEY PROPERTY	AT YOUR OWN BIRTHDAY PARTY	IN A NIGHTCLUB
AT A LIBRARY	ANYWHERE PLAYING CELINE DION / WHITNEY HOUSTON / ADELE	IN THE GROCERY STORE WITH A FULL CART	AT KARAOKE	IN A DOCTOR'S OFFICE

Color in the experiences you've graced with your tears either intentionally or unexpectedly. You'll probably end up winning again, and again, and again (and again).

"SOMETIMES,
only one person is missing
and THE WHOLE WORLD
seems depopulated."

—Alphonse de Lamartine
Méditations Poétiques

Trigger Days

---

*ENDURING—AND REDEFINING—ANNIVERSARIES,
HALLMARK HOLIDAYS, AND MILESTONES*

Anniversary Season

I GET CHILLS WHEN mid-August rolls around, despite the oppressive late-summer temperatures. My body begins to brace itself not just for changing weather but for what I call "anniversary season." The last time I hugged my mom. The last silly, ignorant laugh we shared. The day she died, September 4, which split my life into "The Before" and "The After." You know what I'm talking about.

We all have dreaded portions of the calendar, looming reminders of what we've lost, or how old someone might be now, or all that our person has missed out on. Sometimes you'll wake up crying and continue for days on end or feeling emotionally heavy or super testy. It's like an alarm clock went off in your body. The body records and remembers trauma, even if you're not actively thinking about it, and it knows on a cellular level when the tough times are coming.

And even though you have a heads-up, the tough times can still slam into you in unexpected or even irritating ways. Grief milestones are cruel time machines. They make us remember exactly what we were doing at that moment back in time, and we can feel it all. Or we might feel nothing at all, and then we feel guilty about the numbness, and around and around we go. Know that the way you are feeling is okay, and whatever you are feeling will change over time.

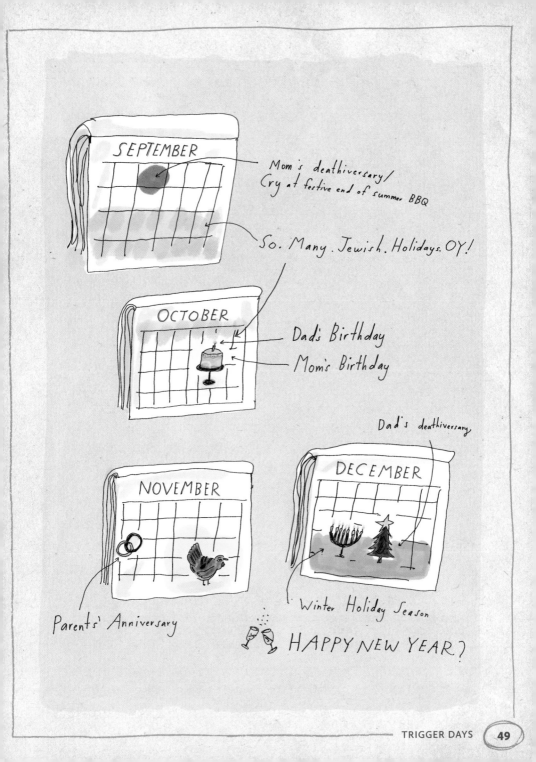

Ideas for the Big Days

Mixing and Matching Welcome

BIRTHDAYS

- **Buy your person a gift and write them a card.** You can always donate or give it to someone who'd appreciate it. Consider buying something for yourself, too—a small token to make you feel like you're going through the motion of gifting something to someone who matters (that'd be you).

- **Make their favorite meal or bake them a cake.** This is also a great opportunity to involve kids in the memory and storytelling process and a way to memorialize your person in a manner that feels celebratory. It also creates space for you to share with others what you loved about your person, their own ways of doing that activity, the way in which you miss them, or what they would have said or thought about recent political and social events, sports, or pop culture.

- **Organize a toast**. Ask people to raise a glass (with you or virtually) to the memory of your person.

- **Spend one day eating their favorite foods** (even if it's cheesecake and tortillas or moonshine and Fritos . . . especially if it's that).

- **Wear something of theirs,** especially the stuff you don't normally put on. That ring, dress, or frayed In-N-Out shirt that's two seconds from disintegrating.

- **Ask people to share memories and anecdotes** that you might no longer have any other way of learning. It's easy to do. Just post a request on social media asking that people either comment or contact you privately, or send a mass bcc'ed email. Include everyone: I once received a fabulous response from my mom's dental hygienist. No idea why she was in my mom's email contacts, but the story was priceless.

- **Do something they always wanted to do but couldn't.** Learn something new that would have delighted them. That card game, magic trick, rafting trip, marathon, museum visit they were too sick to make, sport they were never well enough to try but enjoyed watching on television— dedicate it to them.

DEATHIVERSARIES, DIAGNOSISVERSARIES, AND BEYOND

It's natural for this day to be really, really hard. After all, you're remembering an exact moment in time in which your person did not survive or in which they learned about an illness that would eventually end their lives as opposed to a holiday or birthday that might be associated with happier memories. In other words, it's a mindfuck.

- **Perform an act of kindness in their honor.** If they were a book lover, donate books to your local elementary school. If they loved animals, volunteer at a local shelter and commit the day to their memory.

- **Visibly mark your mourning.** Victorian black and rended shirts aren't the only ways to do this. Consider a memorial tattoo (we have many beautiful examples of them on the Modern Loss website), a daring new hair color, a nose ring, or just wearing something that feels meaningful to you.

- **Reconnect with their crew.** Do you miss your person's close group of friends? It's normal for some of them to fade away after a death—yet another one of those painful secondary losses. This is an excellent opportunity to reconnect. You miss your person; they surely miss them, too. Acknowledge the immortality of love by inviting them to a meal or drinks in your person's memory. Gather somewhere they'd have chosen, whether it's their go-to restaurant, over two-for-one Bud Lites at the biker bar, or a cozy living room.

- **Give an object new meaning.** For example, if you have items that belonged to, were worn by, or might have been worn by your child, ask if you can give them to a friend or an acquaintance who is expecting a child, then have a little send-off. One of our readers had a massive stuffed sheep that comforted her young son when he was dying. One year she and her family took it to FedEx, where they hugged the sheep and cried, then sent it toward its new home: that of a friend who had just given birth after trying for a long time.
- **Master the art of distraction.** What does the trick? Work? Video games? *Ted Lasso*? Cooking? Batting cage? Do it.

TIPS TO GET YOU THROUGH

- **Be intentional.** Some years, you might want to make big plans; others, ignore the day altogether. Don't let anyone else pressure you into feeling a certain way or making a certain plan. It's okay to say no to events organized by others who were close to your person or make a quick appearance before peacing out and getting back to the business of taking care of you.
- **Write a letter to your person**. Fill them in on your life since they've been gone. Catch them up on the stuff you might have talked about over lunch, in bed, or on FaceTime. Tell them about your day, what you're sad they're missing, what you're glad they've missed (bad politicians, global pandemics, etc.), and anything else big or small you wish you could share.

- **Assign yourself a grief buddy.** Ask someone you know who has experienced loss to support you for the day, either virtually or IRL. A lot of people would probably love to be helpful by making space for you on a significant or painful day.

- **Manage your online intake.** This is especially important in advance of all those Hallmark days and traditional holiday periods. You can temporarily opt out of potentially triggering newsletters (Mother's Day onslaught, anyone?), adjust your online ad settings, and unfollow any brands whose marketing campaigns feel like torture. Consider also just *getting offline entirely*, as we all know that the Internet can be one huge trigger when you're feeling raw.

- **Remember that every year feels different.** *This, too, shall pass*, remember? If this time around is particularly hard, it doesn't mean every year will be.

LET THE DAY BE THE DAY

No matter how many advance plans you make for a birthday, holiday, or other glaring date that you worry might flatten you, it's possible you'll wake up wanting to do something completely different. So, here's the best advice I ever received: Let the day be the day.

Don't feel like schlepping up a mountain and honoring your person with a song at the peak? Thought you could handle the family holiday dinner but just cannot bring yourself to show up? No problem, crabby. Pivot! Maybe you'd rather watch all the *Rocky* movies because your person loved them (even *Rocky V*, the worst of them all). Or go to one of those places where you can hurl an axe at the wall. Or take things hour by hour. It's nice to have a plan in your back pocket, but allow yourself to completely change the script. Remember, you're the screenwriter.

PERMISSION SLIP

Tear this out and mail (or send a photo) to any relative or friend who needs to hear you're taking a pass on the "celebrations" this time around. If they have a problem with it, send them to me.

- -

Dear _____,
            THEIR NAME

This gives _____ permission to completely ignore
              YOUR NAME

_____ in the name of taking care of
INSERT TRADITIONAL HOLIDAY/SPECIAL OCCASION HERE

their physical and psychological needs. Grief is hard and unpredict-

able. Everyone will have to deal.

Signed,

MODERN LOSS

CREATIVE WAYS TO MEMORIALIZE
AND MAINTAIN CONNECTION

1. **Little Free Library.** Join the world's largest book-sharing movement and buy one for your community or another one (or organization) in need. Dedicate it to your person's memory, fill it with their favorite books or ones that are reminiscent of their interests and values, and hold an inauguration ceremony of any size.

2. **Phone of the Wind.** In 2010, Itaru Sasaki, a garden designer in Ōtsuchi, built this outside his home so that he could "call" his dead cousin. The next year, a tenth of the city's population was killed in a tsunami, and his phone of the wind ended up becoming a meaningful place of connection for thousands of grievers. While expressing your feelings into a disconnected phone may seem odd, creative outlets like these can help to create space for acceptance and physical and emotional release. Buy an old rotary phone, mount it somewhere peaceful, and dial when you need to. Dedicate it to your person, and make it a communal thing.

3. **Embrace a cause.** Make a list of people or causes you can support, such as running a race to raise money for research, volunteering with animals, or starting a club. It can be anything that makes you truly feel motivated and connected to your person, but it should align with your own interests and strengths (no need to force yourself to do an

Iron Man in honor of your runner when you can barely walk a mile—that's just . . . ridiculous).

4. **Primal release.** Designate a friend to be your scream room or dance party partner (complete with with janky disco ball). Call them and just shout into the phone after giving fair warning. Or insist they play the same Dua Lipa song on repeat while you flail around the living room. The body remembers, and sometimes you need to give that body a break from all its remembering.

Ritual

WHY IS RITUAL IMPORTANT? In times of transition, disconnection, fear, uncertainty, and grief, ritual provides us with something to hang on to for dear life. It's the rope that helps us pull ourselves out of the well, the attention to thought and emotion focused around a particular idea, moment, or individual. Rituals create patterns of thinking, feeling, and doing that ground us in the world we're in, even if our person is gone. They force us to be intentional, even briefly, and offer a wide range of expression and interpretation within a safe moment of opening and closing.

Ritual allows us to literally reframe experience. When you put a new frame on something, it looks different, and that's the point. Grief is a many-angled thing, and so, too, can be its rituals; you might just need to try a few frames. The creative opportunities are endless, and the comfort they provide can be enormous.

If the word *ritual* conjures up public religious rites such as shivas, wakes, and shraddhas, as beautiful as those are, please know that the traditional methods aren't always the most resonant when it comes to grief. Rituals can be hugely personal and private; they can include a handful of people or just you. Rituals are about exploration with no predetermined end goal; we can exercise our agency without attachment to any outcome, and this can help us feel acknowledged (even just by ourselves). They can look like exercises following a particular proven template, or they can be daily writing practices, a party you throw every year, or a place you visit on anniversaries to remember and reflect.

Here are a few I love:

MIZUKO KUYŌ

In Western culture, there is no go-to ritual to address the particularly excruciating grief of pregnancy loss. This Buddhist practice is a memorial service for those who have experienced a miscar-
riage, stillbirth, or abortion. *Kuyō* rituals are an ancient format of Japanese Buddhist practice. But *kuyō* for *mizuko*, which literally means "water child," was developed after World War II, when the Japanese abortion rate rose significantly as a result of a combination of increased legal access, a postwar pregnancy boom, and a postwar recession.

The ceremony consists of an offering made to a small stone statue representing the bodhisattva (enlightened being) *Jizo*, the protector of children, before it is displayed in the temple's yard. The ritual may be a one-time act or may be repeated monthly or annually, and it can be a meaningful thing to bring any living siblings to. Many bereaved parents have found comfort in this ritual for their specific type of loss, still known as the "silent sorrow," which leaves them struggling to figure out how to grieve a child who was never born or one who was never held, named, or took a breath.

DÍA DE MUERTOS

The more you live alongside the reality of death, the more you can accept it. Eventually, it becomes easier to incorporate happiness into living with loss and mourning. This holiday is celebrated on November 1 and 2 primarily in Mexico and throughout Latin America, and I love it because it celebrates death as a part of the human experience.

Life and death are inextricably intertwined. Tradition holds that the dead would be offended by grieving and sadness, so *Día de Muertos* festivities honor them with laughter and joy. The holiday can be applied to remembering anyone, human or animal, and is framed within the context of celebrating, not mourning.

If you're going by the book, you can go to the cemetery to clean and decorate your person's grave (if they have one), then stay for a celebration with objects and activities they enjoyed in life, like food, drink, and music. If you want to do an in-home ceremony, create an altar, or *ofrenda*, which is a table filled with pictures, candles, and objects that tell your person's story. Yes, that

 includes your dad's AC/DC LP or your boyfriend's favorite Al Green shirt or your friend's bong fashioned out of a dented can of Fat Tire. It can bring a sense of tremendous healing.

While you can make an *ofrenda* for yourself, honoring the ones you've lost—setting out their favorite foods, books, objects, an old pair of running shoes you can't throw out—you can also involve others in your altar. Maybe a friend just lost their brother; ask what he most liked to eat, then include it. Anything can belong in an *ofrenda*, and it is your defined ritualistic space over which you have full control. (Watch *Coco* for inspiration.)

THE BESPOKE HOLIDAY

I'm admittedly someone who is given to hyperbole, but this is truly my favorite of many favorite ideas. Creating your own holiday can be one of the most joyful and meaningful rituals through which you connect to your person. And if you don't believe that quite literally anything goes in this grand experiment, may I offer Festivus as an example? Not only is it a made-up secular holiday *from a sitcom*, but its primary activity is complaining, and its only decoration is an unadorned aluminum pole, for Pete's sake.

Here are two I participate in each year:

The Dave Johns Memorial Big Mac Day

My friend Amanda Johns Perez's dad died from cancer shortly after she graduated college. Every December 15, his death day, she posts her favorite photo of him, in which he smiles widely while prepping something very tasty looking from the home bar, and asks people to celebrate his memory alongside her by indulging in his favorite fast-food guilty pleasure (other acceptable choices include Filet-O-Fish, Bombay Sapphire martinis, and scotch and soda—anything that's kind of bad for you, really). Needless to say, everyone looks forward to Dave Johns Memorial Big Mac Day. Over the years, a growing number of celebrants share photos of the copious amounts of crap we let ourselves eat and drink in his name, along with a toast to him and the amazing daughter he produced who managed to turn an enormously painful date into something to look forward to.

Katie Fisher Day

Katie was an avid baker who sent her brother—my friend Matt—fresh-baked cookies every week when he was at college. Katie died in a car accident at twenty-four. Two years later, Matt and his friends from the comedy community founded Katie Fisher Day to commemorate her outsized warmth and affection. Each year on March 12, her birthday, they bake cookies for a loved one in memory of Katie, the brilliant engineer and dancer who lit up the room wherever she went. Everyone involved promotes it on social media, and people everywhere send cookies and share stories of loved ones. Matt has received photos of baked goods care packages from Norway, Russia, Uganda, and more. The best? Whenever he searches #katiefisherday on Facebook or Twitter, he can see how people took the time to make their love active and tangible, just like Katie did.

Which rituals could you create? Brainstorm here.

_____

_____

_____

The Less Pithy but Way More Accurate Stages of Grief

Disclaimer: Sometimes you'll go through all of these in the same day.

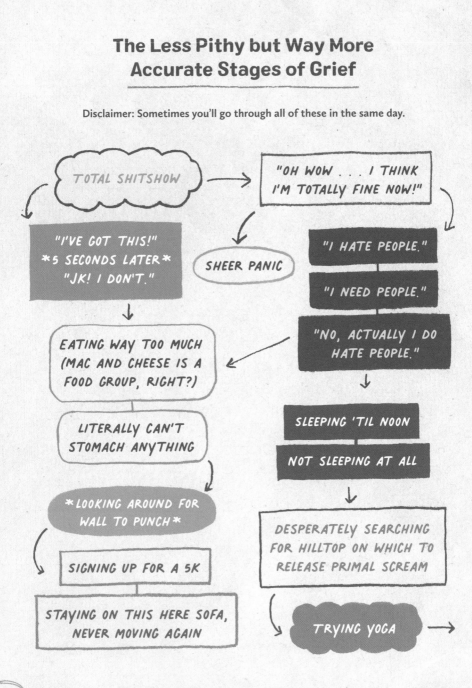

TOTAL SHITSHOW

"OH WOW . . . I THINK I'M TOTALLY FINE NOW!"

"I'VE GOT THIS!" *5 SECONDS LATER* "JK! I DON'T."

SHEER PANIC

"I HATE PEOPLE."

"I NEED PEOPLE."

"NO, ACTUALLY I DO HATE PEOPLE."

EATING WAY TOO MUCH (MAC AND CHEESE IS A FOOD GROUP, RIGHT?)

LITERALLY CAN'T STOMACH ANYTHING

SLEEPING 'TIL NOON

NOT SLEEPING AT ALL

LOOKING AROUND FOR WALL TO PUNCH

SIGNING UP FOR A 5K

STAYING ON THIS HERE SOFA, NEVER MOVING AGAIN

DESPERATELY SEARCHING FOR HILLTOP ON WHICH TO RELEASE PRIMAL SCREAM

TRYING YOGA

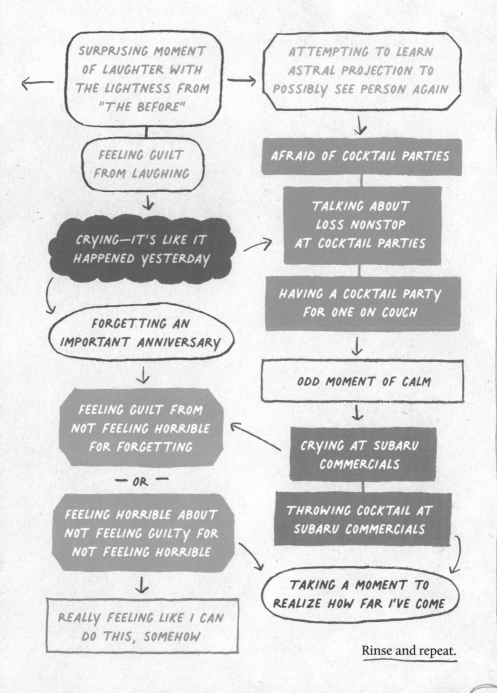

Rinse and repeat.

Word Jumble

How many words can you make out of the letters in . . .

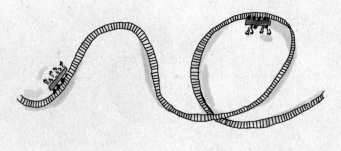

EMOTIONAL ROLLERCOASTER

LAME ELECTORAL

STELLAR TACO

"What would taking care of your pain look like? Like allowing it to be pain. Normal, ordinary pain that is the by-product of abnormal extraordinary loss. BEFORE IT EBBS, IT HAS TO RAGE. Anything else is a lack of health."

—Kate Inglis

Help Is on the Way

HOW TO GET IT AND GIVE IT TO YOURSELF

Formal Therapy:
Why, What's Out There, and How to Look for It

GRIEF ISN'T PATHOLOGICAL. When someone meaningful dies, it impacts everything. There's nothing "wrong" with you. No one person or thing can fix our suffering or quicken the process of moving through our grief. Just like anything else in life, there's no magic wand, pill, or saying that will disappear grief, but of course you'll wish it could be otherwise. In terms of your long-term health and happiness, however, it's worth accepting that the kindest way to grieve is to allow yourself to slow down, access and acknowledge the tough stuff, and then work through it.

But as we do, we need an ally or allies who will sit with us, listen with a calm, empathic, and trained ear, and help us figure out ways to help ourselves. People heal best when they're allowed to tell their stories to witnesses (often professionals) willing to hear them. If you're gonna feel the feelings, you might as well feel them with someone who won't be rattled and who's schooled in strategies that can help you examine and cope with them.

While I believe in the utter and epic power of friendship, peer-to-peer support, and even this handbook, I also believe the right therapist can work wonders when folded into the rest of your support mechanisms, even if you feel like you're doing fine in the moment. Just as you brush your teeth to prevent cavities, it's vitally important, especially when made vulnerable by grief, to care for your emotional well-being in the same way you'd tend to your physical health—ideally, before a mental health crisis. In short, and especially for those who were raised to view therapy as a way to "fix" something gone awry in your personality, regular therapy can help you avoid sinking into a grief hole that sucks the joy out of your existence.

Within this section, you'll find some reasons to consider grief therapy or seek support from a dedicated professional. This is a guide to finding the right practitioner for you and your specific needs as well as a primer on some of the therapies[1] that have helped members of the Modern Loss community.

SIX REASONS TO TRY GRIEF THERAPY

1. **Claim your own personal space without apology.** Life is busy. And while we excel at finding time to watch an entire season of *Hacks* in one weekend, we're impressively bad at placing "create the space to reflect on some real stuff" high on our priority list. We need to accept our losses in order to address them. But we can't address them if we don't admit what they are. A therapy session is a designated place to do just that. It forces you to be present in the moment with someone skilled in active listening and who knows what to listen for. These days, any corner can turn into a therapy setting. (During Covid-19, mine took place via FaceTime sessions in my car, the only place I could get any privacy while on lockdown.)

[1] The purpose of this book is not to provide therapy, so I'm offering short descriptions of various modalities that have helped our community, though of course many more exist. I encourage you to do further research into any one that seems like it might be worth trying.

2. **It's a safe testing ground.** Your sessions are the perfect setting to get ideas for new tools, try them out, talk through which ones are working for you, and get suggestions on new ones as needed. A therapist will also know whether to encourage you to continue with any of these for a bit longer if you seem prematurely ready to reject them. They should teach you how to use a compass, not give you a map (spoiler alert: there aren't any).

3. **You're paying someone to listen to you.** A therapist's job is to sit with you, guide you through questions, and help you come up with your *own* conclusions about what you need. As much as I would have loved this during various points in my own grief therapy, they aren't there to "fix" a situation or tell you what you absolutely *must* do—and you should be wary of or avoid any who do. If you want that approach, save the money and call your most opinionated relative, who will happily offer their two cents, unsolicited or otherwise.

4. **You can be completely unfiltered.** All those façades you put on to make it through work, home life, dinner with friends, the bagel place, and maybe even looking in the mirror? The masks that feel so exhausting to keep on? They can stay off in your sessions without concern or embarrassment. There's no need to keep it together or worry about how what you will say will affect them. Fly your flag. They can take it. (And they want to.)

5. **Nobody else has the floor.** The right therapist is on your team (and there is only one team present here). They have your back 100 percent. Your session gives you a set time and place to regularly express your emotions in an unfiltered way without any fear of conflict of

interest present (like another family member or friend with particular sensitivities or with whom you don't get along). It becomes a routine that you fit into your life, a time that is just for and decided by you. Want to reminisce? Complain about what a pain in the ass your person could be? Gripe about how your brother is driving you absolutely insane during the estate process? This is your relief valve.

6. **It's never too late to seek support.** Because there's no time limit on grieving, there's no time limit on starting grief therapy. Six weeks, six months, six years . . . regardless of how much time has passed, it's always worth taking a look at the impact grief has had on your well-being and steps you might take to feel better, more regulated, and more hopeful about whatever comes next for you.

FINDING THE RIGHT FIT

Well-meaning people in your life may have suggestions for types of counseling that worked for them and that you *absolutely must* try. Well, first, therapists aren't typically shared among close friends and family, but those practitioners might be able to recommend someone to you. And just because someone had success with that person or method doesn't mean that either will be right for your particular grief-related experience. You are unique, your grief is unique, ergo, the alchemy each person has with a therapist? *Ding-ding-ding*, also unique. Your therapy is custom fit to you; it's "emotional couture," if you will (and yes, you should absolutely start sharing that phrase). Try to speak with a few different people, and go with your gut.

A note on patience and trust:

Ultimately, it's about finding someone who understands you and who you feel you can trust with the most private and difficult thoughts and experiences of your life. They don't have to be like you to understand you and treat you with respect. Nobody will ever fully understand your grief, but a therapist wants to try. That's empathy.

The concept of trust is loaded when it comes to starting therapy. You're probably not going to spill it all to a stranger right away (even a therapist!), and building trust in the therapy relationship is akin to building trust in our other ones. It takes time. If you're someone with trust issues, it may take more time, and that's okay. A good therapist won't pressure or push you to overshare or enter territory that may feel like a violation of your boundaries. You're interviewing them for a job, and you should ask them about the lengths of sessions, the frequency they recommend for you, missed appointment policies, how interactive the sessions will be, and whatever else you're curious about.

You'll only know if you'll connect with someone when you finally sit down with them, but remember that you can always make a change. You can't control grief, but in this instance, you are in charge. Exercising this agency can be, in itself, a positive step forward.

WHAT TO CONSIDER WHEN LOOKING FOR A THERAPIST

Write down what you'd feel comfortable with to help with your research.

What is their training background (e.g., PhD, PsyD, LCSW, LMFT, LMHC, MD)? What are their specialties (e.g., CBT, EMDR, psychodynamic, integrative, psychiatry, etc.)? Do they specialize in counseling, clinical, marriage or couples/family counseling, or social work?

_____

_____

_____

_____

How do they work with grieving clients? Do they view grief as a process you'll go through in some form for the rest of your life or as something that is constricted to a timeline? In a world where there is a tendency to pathologize normal grief reactions, it's important to find people who are "grief informed."

_____

_____

_____

_____

_____

_____

Cost: Are they in your healthcare plan? Can you afford it (and if not, can you get outside financial assistance)? Do they offer sliding-scale fees?

_____

_____

_____

_____

_____

Availability and accessibility: Do you need early morning or evening? Is their location close to work or home, or can you work together remotely? Will they offer emergency sessions or allow you to text or email them in between seeing each other?

_____

_____

_____

_____

_____

Political beliefs

_____

_____

_____

_____

Cultural background: Do you want someone who can understand your ethnic and cultural background, sexual orientation, gender identity/expression, faith/spirituality? Will they give any biased feedback on any of these that could make you uncomfortable?

_____

_____

_____

_____

_____

_____

_____

_____

_____

_____

_____

_____

Age

_____

Gender identity (male, female, nonbinary, etc.)

_____

Forms of Therapy

THERE ARE A LOT OUT THERE, but here are the primary types that have helped Modern Loss community members, including ones that many of our therapeutic advisory board members focus on.

TALK THERAPY

This is a term used to describe general psychotherapy that relies on—you guessed it!—talking to help clients work through challenges. People struggling with a range of emotional difficulties can work toward understanding themselves better, identifying problematic patterns of behavior, and alleviating emotional symptoms. There are many different types of talk therapy, such as psychodynamic psychotherapy, cognitive behavioral therapy, humanistic psychotherapy, dialectical behavioral therapy, and so on. But not every therapist is "grief trained," and it's worth finding someone who is.

How Can It Help with Grief?

Talk therapy provides a safe, confidential place to explore all aspects of loss. It's the therapist's job to support you, listen objectively, and provide empathic, practical feedback that will hopefully help you learn and grow into a good life after loss. This is the place where the underbelly of the relationship with your person can be unearthed without judgment, platitudes, or pressure to not feel things that may be stigmatized or judged by the mainstream. Sometimes, family and friends can't tolerate anything but idealization of the dead, but no relationship can exist without ambivalence. Talk therapy is a great space to process and work through it all.

So. Many. Options. How Do I Decide?

Try not to go down the rabbit hole about which type of talk therapy to seek. Above all else, the therapeutic relationship is what matters most. If your therapist doesn't feel like a good match, you won't get anywhere. Look for someone with whom you can build a trusting, collaborative working relationship. Follow your intuition.

COGNITIVE BEHAVIORAL THERAPY (CBT)

CBT focuses on the relationship between thoughts, behaviors, and feelings. Your therapist will teach you techniques to examine, challenge, and reduce unhelpful thinking, behaviors, and emotional patterns.

Why Should I Try It?

CBT isn't typically the first step in grief therapy, but it can be helpful to manage some of the symptoms that can stem from grief and is frequently used as part of an integrated approach alongside other therapies. CBT is the most widely used therapy for anxiety disorders and can be effective in the treatment of panic disorder, phobias, social and generalized anxiety disorder, among other conditions.

EYE MOVEMENT DESENSITIZATION AND REPROCESSING (EMDR)

EMDR is a trauma therapy that alleviates emotional distress associated with disturbing memories that might be causing flashbacks, loss of a sense of control, and other issues that can negatively impact someone's daily life and ability to function. It's based on the idea that a memory that hasn't been properly integrated into the mind can get stuck in raw form, with the emotions, physical sensations, and negative things we felt at the very moment of that experience remaining relatively unchanged.

As my own therapist described it to me when I did EMDR years ago, if you're playing a record that keeps skipping, the process helps to adjust the needle so that the song can continue to play. Here's an example: Let's say you were in a car accident and are stuck in the trauma of the experience. EMDR's goal is to get you to appreciate that you had a traumatic experience while also realizing "What happened was terrifying. It's amazing that I survived."

How Is It Different from Talk Therapy?

EMDR focuses on alleviating symptoms stemming from trauma. It can be a great complement to your primary therapy by addressing points you are stuck on.

Ideally, your practitioner will teach you some strategies used during the sessions so that you can employ them whenever you need to calm your body and your mind. These include grounding, tapping, mindfulness, and relaxation exercises (check out some ideas for these on page 116).

GROUP THERAPY

Grief support groups aren't for everyone. But one huge benefit is in the universality of experience felt within the group. Nobody can ever know exactly what it's like to be experiencing *your* grief as *you*, but common themes that emerge in groups can help to lighten the deep sense of aloneness that accompanies grief. This is particularly helpful for people grieving stigmatized or politicized losses, such as drug overdoses, suicide, murder, AIDS-related illness, stillbirth and infant loss, miscarriage and terminating a pregnancy for medical reasons (TFMR), medically assisted euthanasia, and Covid-19.

Some Types of Group Therapy:

◉ **Open v. closed:** You can join the former at any time versus the entire group starting the session together. With an open group, there may be an adjustment period while you get to know the other participants. With a closed group, you might need to wait several months until you find one that feels like a fit.

◉ Specific to age and type of loss

◉ **Process groups v. agenda driven:** Process groups focus on the group experience, and leaders serve more as facilitators than instructors. Members participate by engaging in group discussions and activities and can lead to a sense of community.

Agenda-driven groups are led by a qualified therapist who sets goals for the sessions and provides members with information about specific issues. In this setting, the therapist provides most of the content.

◉ **Socializing v. not socializing outside of the group:** Some groups ask members to refrain from socializing outside of sessions. Others encourage it. Regardless, all members must agree to protect the identities of fellow members, keep the content of each session confidential, and refrain from discussing another member's personal history with anyone else.

The DIYs

The opposite of war is not peace, it's CREATION."

— Jonathan Larson, Rent

THERE ARE SO MANY creative and artistic tools for processing thoughts and emotions that erupt during grief and continue during its aftermath. While not a substitute for formal therapy, in the throes of an experience that gives you very little sense of control, these projects can provide you with some. You get to choose the timing, medium, creative process, end point, and so on. You can share them or keep them to yourself—and these activities go way beyond simple journaling. You get to exercise your agency. Doing so helps put a frame around the chaos, even if momentarily.

MAKE PLAYLISTS

Music can be an excellent tool in managing grief and building coping skills. Understanding how music affects you and which songs trigger particular memories and emotions can have a substantive impact on reclaiming a bit of stability in your loss and building resilience.

Certain notes in a certain order can form a powerful time machine. A song playing in the grocery store as you innocuously compare Keto-approved products may churn up such intense mental and sensory feelings of a certain time, place, or experience that you're suddenly somewhere else in your brain, even though your body is left crying in Aisle 4.

Especially in the raw stages of early grief, it can be beneficial to create various playlists to use in regulating emotions. Build some out on this page, starting with your own music collection, and go from there.

Energize

Songs to help motivate you to clean up, get dressed, and get going.

NAME	NAME
ARTIST	ARTIST

NAME	NAME
ARTIST	ARTIST

NAME	NAME
ARTIST	ARTIST

NAME	NAME
ARTIST	ARTIST

NAME	NAME
ARTIST	ARTIST

Relax and Regulate

Songs to help soothe and comfort.

_____ NAME _____ ARTIST	_____ NAME _____ ARTIST
_____ NAME _____ ARTIST	_____ NAME _____ ARTIST
_____ NAME _____ ARTIST	_____ NAME _____ ARTIST
_____ NAME _____ ARTIST	_____ NAME _____ ARTIST
_____ NAME _____ ARTIST	_____ NAME _____ ARTIST

Rage On

Intense songs to help the anger and anxiety move through and out of your body.

NAME	NAME
ARTIST	ARTIST

NAME	NAME
ARTIST	ARTIST

NAME	NAME
ARTIST	ARTIST

NAME	NAME
ARTIST	ARTIST

NAME	NAME
ARTIST	ARTIST

New Stuff

Discover some music that you don't associate with your person. Ask people whose taste you respect for suggestions. Download stuff you've never heard before. Tap those recommendations popping up on Spotify or Apple Music. Use the tracks you gravitate to as the soundtrack to the new sense of self and existence you are building in your post-loss universe.

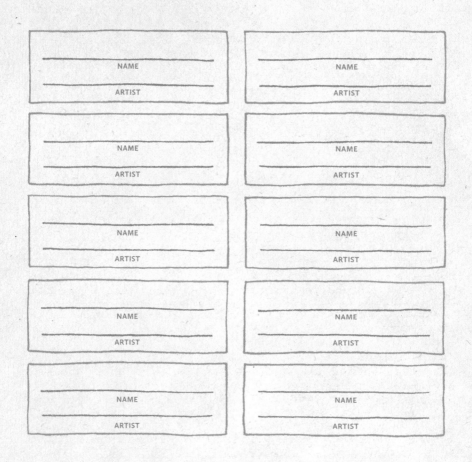

NAME

ARTIST

NAME

ARTIST

NAME

ARTIST

NAME

ARTIST

NAME

ARTIST

NAME

ARTIST

NAME

ARTIST

NAME

ARTIST

NAME

ARTIST

NAME

ARTIST

Steer Clear

What songs bring up difficult emotions and reactions? Any that trigger intense sadness and a feeling of being overwhelmed can be put in a mental lockbox for now. You'll know where to find them if you really want to.

NAME ARTIST	NAME ARTIST
NAME ARTIST	NAME ARTIST
NAME ARTIST	NAME ARTIST
NAME ARTIST	NAME ARTIST
NAME ARTIST	NAME ARTIST

SMASH SOMETHING

You know what feels great sometimes? Breaking shit.

Remember the film *Office Space*? The scene when, after yet another paper jam, the characters yank a continually malfunctioning printer/copier/fax machine from the wall, toss it in the car, drive it to the middle of a field, and attack it with baseball bats with such gusto while the Geto Boys' "Still" screams, "Die, motherfuckers! Die!" that even the viewer experiences catharsis? You, too, can have that feeling.

While going through your person's belongings, did you find a box full of chipped or cracked mugs? An overabundance of lightbulbs that nobody could possibly use? An ancient Okidata Microline 320 Turbo Mono DOT matrix printer? (Oh, you didn't? I found two.) Use it as an opportunity to get some feelings out. Find a large box or bucket, toss on some protective glasses, and just smash it to pieces. Really listen to the shattering glass and ceramic as you throw down your feelings of anger and despair. Then, make some art! Set the pieces in a concrete mold to make stepping stones for your garden, or grout them to the sides of a terra-cotta pot to make a new home for that plant your friend sent when your mom died.

When Gabi and I launched Modern Loss, we heard about a store in Japan selling only plain white plates that you purchase and promptly hurl at a wall. Since then, several places have popped up around the world that let you similarly channel your feelings into cathartic destruction. IMHO, they're doing God's work. Go find one, and please invite me to join.

NOW, MAKE SOME STUFF

Rip these platitudes into pieces, then make a collage on the next page. (Proud of your final product? Post it to social media and tag @modernloss.)

COLLAGE ME!

REUSE AND REPURPOSE

We often don't know what to do with our dead person's clothes. I mean, who needs thirty-seven stained graphic tees? Select a few of your favorites and make reusable bags. Simply cut off the collar and sleeves, sew up the bottom, and take it to the farmers' market to fill with fresh bread and produce. Ask a crafty friend to make a quilt out of your husband's dress shirts. Cut your sister's skinny jeans into long strips, and braid or sew them into a denim rug (no, I don't know how to do this either, but that's what TikTok is for). Donate some of the baby clothes that

remind you of your child, and imagine them having a new life on a different little body. Find functional ways to bring the clothing they loved into your everyday life. But don't let yourself be pressured into doing so until you feel ready.

BUY AN ART SET

Having good-quality art supplies at your disposal can be beneficial in supporting your grief process. A set of watercolor paints, paper, brushes, colored pencils, and pens are excellent tools to keep on the coffee table to take out when the mood strikes. Paint and draw whatever you need to express, be it a peaceful focusing activity or an angry, moody expression, without worrying about the quality of your artistry. Store your creations in a journal or portfolio, and document the day, time, emotions, and thoughts behind them on the back of each one.

CREATE A BOOK

Books are a safe way to explore big feelings, not only by reading but also by writing them. Before you freak out thinking I'm suggesting you pen the next *Year of Magical Thinking*, remember that a book is any number of pages bound between two covers. Whatever number that is and whatever is on those pages is up to you. It could be a graphic novel, a book of poetry (including haikus), a simple memory or fantasy, or anything in between.

Here is a short creative process altered from a piece that Caron Levis wrote for Modern Loss. Caron should know; she's the author of several picture books, including *Ida, Always*, one of my favorite titles on loss, which I've read to my kids for years. This piece was originally geared toward working with children, but let's be honest: Grown-ups have a lot of big feelings, too (raises hand).

1. **Prepare.** Before starting, read some published stories on loss, and identify your support systems and resources.
2. **Create structure.** Do you want to create an illustrated story, a graphic narrative, just text?
3. **Choose a focus.** What part of the story needs to be explored? Do you need a way to celebrate your person? A space in which to share worries or fears? Explore feelings around past events that feel complicated or confusing? Simply document special memories or events? Once you decide, write that story. Include challenging memories along with the positive ones to allow your person to be fully human and allow space for complicated feelings. Ask yourself what sights, sounds, smells, foods, places, objects, holidays, events, and dialogue are associated with the narrative.

4. **Create a hopeful ending.** Just as in real life, you don't want anyone minimizing your loss with platitudes, you probably don't want a book about loss splattered with rainbow unicorns and bows, so think hopeful rather than happy for your ending. Hope can be found in nature, future adventures, memories, places or activities that make you happy, and the people who love us, to name a few. Hopefulness doesn't mean that the skies are once again a pure periwinkle blue, but hope being present can have a strong effect.

5. **Put it together.** Your book can be as simple as stapled drawing paper and crayons or as crafty as collage, glitter glue, laminators, and design software and apps.

6. **Share it (if you want).** Sharing your story in the right setting can promote a sense of connection. Depending on the final narrative, you might decide to keep the book to yourself. Or you might want to share it with friends and family you trust. Communicating about a loss is essential, but so is the choice of with whom, when, and how much you want to share it.

7. **Reflect.** Think about how you felt going through this process. Want to do it again in a similar way? Explore a different angle? Go for it. (And congratulations! You're officially an author.)

MAKE A MEMORY BOX

Chances are your person left behind *a lot of stuff*. And laying among all that stuff are ephemera difficult to part with because they represent so much of them (like the handwritten registration form I found for my mom's fourth—fourth!—consecutive beginner's bridge class). As someone living in a very small, very cluttered apartment when my mom died, I appreciated being exposed to projects like these, where I could go to the storage unit I'd rented for all her things and combine a sanity-saving activity with generating a meaningful thing I could give to the people in her life who loved her nearly as much as I did.

Tear some pages from your person's favorite books and pull some damaged photo prints, then make a collage on a wooden or cardboard box. Use the box to store pictures, notes, ticket stubs, and tokens that hold sentimental value. Make some for other people, and if you have kids, create some for them, too, with magical discoveries awaiting beneath the lid. Or display items in glass containers around your home and change out the contents on a rotating basis. You are Chief Curator of the Museum of Your Person.*

Special thanks to Modern Loss contributor RoseAnna Cyr, MA, MT-BC, LMHC, for advising on this section. RoseAnna is a licensed clinical mental health counselor, music therapist, and school counselor.

*I also want to relieve you of any guilt associated with getting rid of belongings. Sometimes they're donated, sometimes they're sold, sometimes they're gifted, and sometimes they're just recycled or trashed. It's all okay.

Write Your Six-Word Memoir

ONE TENET OF MODERN LOSS is that storytelling is a change agent. But it doesn't always have to take place in the form of a memoir, personal essay, or even long conversation. Sometimes, storytelling can effectively happen in just a few words.

My friend Larry Smith popularized the use of the six-word story by asking his *SMITH Magazine* community to describe their lives in exactly—you guessed it—six words. His website has now published more than a million of these short slices of life on every topic imaginable—love, immigration, childhood, food, hope, and the list goes on.

This form is so popular because it's a wonderfully democratic way of storytelling. A 3-year-old can do it, and a 103-year-old can do it. It allows you to tell a sliver of your story—just enough to create intrigue and spark a conversation and connection with someone else. But beyond that, I've found it's the perfect way to crack open people's thinking when it comes to loss. Grief is a topic that is overwhelming, scary, and oftentimes traumatizing; we shouldn't require that someone write a thousand words on the experience to deeply access and process their feelings on the matter.

In the months leading up to Modern Loss's launch in 2013, Larry and I shared a mountain of fries in Greenwich Village. I made him promise that as soon as Modern Loss was actually a thing, he would partner with us to produce a live Six Words on Loss storytelling event. I'm not sure if he really believed that I'd successfully figure out how to actually put a site online (I surely had my doubts), but he humored me and said yes. Two years later, we held our first live event at the New York City-based headquarters of the media company Refinery29, and a tradition was born.

Since then, Modern Loss has produced large-scale, live six-word story shows around the United States featuring *Saturday Night Live* "Weekend Update" writer Katie Rich, *The Late Show with Stephen Colbert*'s Steve Waltien, writer Ashley C. Ford, the late *Sex and the City* actor Willie Garson, *Forever35* podcast host Kate Spencer, *GIRLS* writer Yassir Lester, and Broadway composer Shaina Taub, to name just a few. We've also done them in more intimate settings, like some of my favorite bookstores around the country, and really, *really* intimate settings, like all the Zooms I led throughout the Covid-19 pandemic for non-profits, corporations, and museums. They are always a mix of moving, hilarious, profound, creative, and inspiring. But more than anything, they always crack open and create community.

So now that you know the backstory behind this exercise, I want you to try it out for yourself. Keep coming back to this page and to add another six-word story whenever you want to meditate on memories, feelings, wishes, or anything that comes to mind about your loss experience.

Here are a few that have been shared at our events:

DEAD MOMS DON'T ATTRACT SINGLE JEWS. (THAT ONE IS MINE... THEY JUST DON'T.)

SHE NEVER GOT TO SEE PARIS.

NOW MY BODY IS ALWAYS TENSE.

NEVER MET YOU. BUT LOVE YOU.

SO NOW I'M AN ONLY CHILD.

There is a vastness to grief that overwhelms our miniscule selves. We are TINY, TREMBLING CLUSTERS OF ATOMS subsumed within grief's awesome presence. It occupies the cove of our being and extends through our fingers to the limits of the universe."
— Nick Cave

The Mind/Body
Grief Continuum

GO WITH THE FLOW

You Can Fool Everyone But Yourself

I'VE BEEN FORTUNATE to run Modern Loss summer retreats at the Kripalu Center for Yoga and Health in the Berkshires alongside Emily Rapp Black. She's an associate professor of creative writing at the University of California-Riverside, where she also teaches medical narratives in the School of Medicine. Emily is intimately acquainted with grief: her son, Ronan, died from Tay-Sachs when he was three.

The attendees have come from all over the United States and Canada for an incomparable opportunity for deep, IRL interactions with people who know what you're going through. When two people who have experienced loss meet for the first time, there's an almost instant emotional shorthand. We recognize one another.

During these retreats, we do a group activity called "Open Space." Everyone gets the chance to convene a session on whatever is on their mind. They name it; they run it. And every time, there is always someone who wants to talk about the havoc grief wreaks on our minds and bodies. Emily coined this session "Body Shit," and everyone always knows exactly what she means by it.

Here's the scoop on the mind and the body and how grief connects them: The body remembers *everything*. We hold our sorrows inside these bodies that move and think and sleep and grieve and cry. But in this culture in which we're encouraged and sometimes expected to grieve for a certain period and have it all done and dusted, move on, and *thank u next*, we learn to put on the proverbial brave face. We think if we push grief down, it will stay down.

Nope. This is why when some people, after a death, are asked, "How are you?" and they say, "I'm fine," they might lock themselves in their car for an hour to scream and cry anyway. Your body might break out in hives, your back might go out, you might get dizzy or feel your heart racing even when you're not exerting yourself. All of this is the body telling you that you need to pay attention to the grief it is containing. Body shit is real because grief is all-consuming. You feel the loss of the body of your person in your body (and if you've read Bessel van der Kolk's *The Body Keeps the Score*, this will all make sense). How could it be otherwise?

But there's this, too: There's no quick fix because there is no fix at all. This doesn't mean you won't feel better. **It means that grief is not a wall to climb over. It's an ever-changing experience you must learn to integrate within yourself.** This new reality, however unwelcome, infuriating, or unfair, means the reality of the loss cannot be sealed off, or much like overfilling the pressure cooker I'm still terrified to use, whatever is inside will probably explode without a safety valve.

But how can you release something if you're pretending it doesn't exist? You can't. You must acknowledge your feelings—the good, the bad, the ugly, the scary, the weird—and instead of labeling them in that fashion, just examine them. Be curious. Get to know your body and what it's trying to tell you. You may not want to hear it, but you need to, and you will be the better for it.

In this section, you'll find a range of practical, tactical activities from my own research and experience, expert opinions, and members of the Modern Loss community that are intended to alleviate some of the mind and body's stress, anxiety, and lack of rest that we suffer from during grief—both in the acute stages and in the years and decades following.

GRIEF EFFECTS

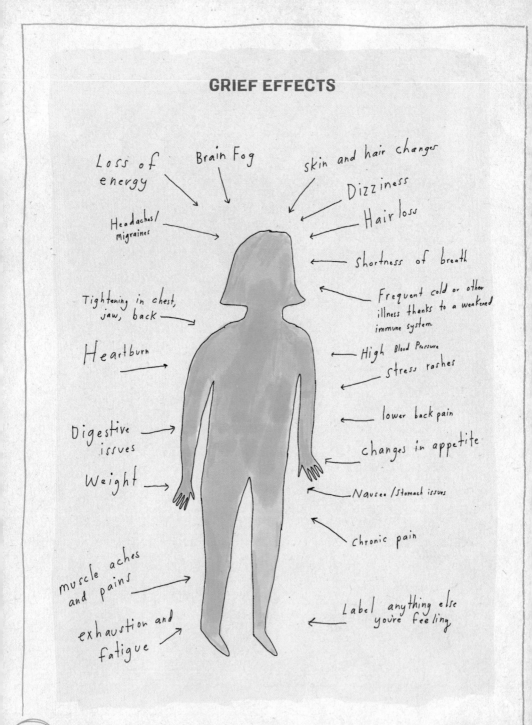

Loss of energy

Brain Fog

skin and hair changes

Dizziness

Hair loss

Headaches/migraines

shortness of breath

Frequent cold or other illness thanks to a weakened immune system.

Tightening in chest, jaw, back

High Blood Pressure

stress rashes

Heartburn

lower back pain

changes in appetite

Digestive issues

Nausea/stomach issues

Weight

Chronic pain

muscle aches and pains

exhaustion and fatigue

Label anything else you're feeling

Sleep, Rest, and Dreams

IF YOU HAVEN'T NOTICED, grief is freaking exhausting. When you're in the throes of it, grief demands the attention of your entire body, mind, and soul. And even afterward, it's still draining. You know how toddlers are totally fried by the witching hour of 4 p.m. because their little minds have been working hard all day trying to figure out the world? Think of yourself as a toddler, especially in early grief, because your brain is, in fact, on overdrive trying to figure out this strange new world.

But as wiped out as you might be, in desperate need of restoration and rest, sleep seems to be the first thing to get completely messed up when life goes sideways. It's a physiological process that is incredibly sensitive to emotional trauma. High levels of stress can mess with your hormones—notably, pushing your cortisol level through the roof—and keep you awake at night. Even if you're grief-sleeping for nine hours straight, it's quite possible you'll still wake up feeling like you just lost at Fight Club and be groggy throughout the day. Unfortunately, sleep is exactly what you need to rise to the mental and physical challenges of this ride.

Unless you reside in an ashram or on a remote high plain, it's impossible to tune out the world—work, current events, home life, your mind. But you're probably capable of attempting at least a couple of the ideas in this section. See what makes a difference with your sleep dysregulation, and go from there.

SLEEP

Some paths to higher-quality overnights:

- Instead of approaching your sleep routine as yet another chore to do in grief-land, try to reframe it as a proactive choice to care for yourself during a difficult time.

- Try to avoid eating at least three hours before bedtime, and limit your caffeine and alcohol intake. If you must work at night, build in wind-down time, and *absolutely do not work in bed*.

- As tempting as it can be to use your bed as a sanctuary, don't—even on days when you wake up and don't want to roll out. Force yourself into a different place of relaxation and slothiness.

- If you're in a position to do so, try having sex or even just snuggling.

- Just. Put. The phone. Down. My friend, you know you shouldn't look at your phone right before bed. And yet you do it anyway, which is why I'm telling you to stop.

- Try some relaxing routines that don't activate your brain *too* much before bed but are also slightly mentally engaging, like coloring or another easy art project, while listening to something with words, such as a podcast, class, or music with lyrics.

Several of the above recommendations are from Anne D. Bartolucci, PhD, CBSM, a behavioral sleep medicine specialist based in Atlanta.

² You get a pass for staying in bed all day on an occasional, as-needed basis.

ORIGAMI

What's that? You were trying to think of a slightly mentally engaging, easy art project? How convenient that I just happen to have a pre-bedtime crab origami project for you right here. Take a few minutes to calmly focus on the simple task of folding a piece of origami paper into the most resilient creature on earth, and display it somewhere to remind you of your own badass crabbiness.

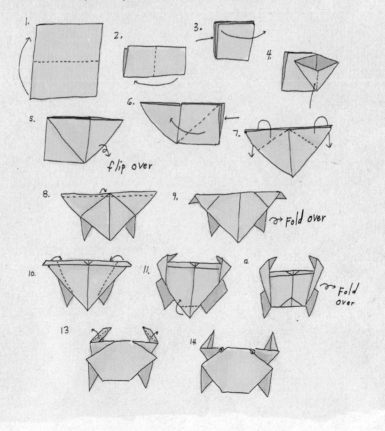

When to Seek Out Help

If sleep starts to become a serious issue that's interfering with your ability to stay safe and generally productive during the day, consider reaching out to a specialist:

PROBLEM: Ongoing insomnia (falling/staying asleep)

SPECIALIST: A sleep medicine doctor. These are MDs with a certification in sleep medicine and can be anyone from a primary care physician or a neurologist with an extra specialty. They can prescribe medication if necessary.

PROBLEM: Are you technically sleeping "enough" but still waking exhausted? Your main problem might be insomnia (falling/staying asleep) or anxiety or nightmares that make you want to avoid bedtime.

SPECIALIST: Behavioral sleep medicine specialist. These are PhDs and PsyDs who are clinical or counseling psychologists with extra certification in behavioral sleep medicine. They may try imagery rehearsal therapy to change the content of your dreams before going to sleep. They do not prescribe medication.

A NOTE ON SLEEP TRACKERS

Consider this before you buy yourself an expensive gadget to record every single detail of your overnight experience: Research shows they can actually make sleep worse. The more you stare at the results, the more you can become obsessed with it and the more anxious you get about it, and do you really need more of that right now?

REST

Regardless of how much sleep you're getting, it's important to carve out time to rest whenever you can throughout the day. Here are some ways to remind yourself to do so:

- Schedule it into your calendar, just as you would a meeting.

- Tell people you can count on to send you reminders to press pause.

- "Go micro" when things are overwhelming.

- Embrace JOMO (the joy of missing out). Get better at telling people when you're too tired to do something. Read this carefully: It's okay to cancel plans. It's okay to say no. It's okay to opt out.

GO MICRO

A cheat sheet for getting through the next hour, week, or minute.

- ☐ MAKE SOMETHING—DRAW, DOODLE, GIVE YOURSELF A MINUTE TO BREATHE.
- ☐ TAKE A QUICK WALK AROUND THE BLOCK.
- ☐ LISTEN TO SOME NATURE SOUNDS.
- ☐ TALK TO YOURSELF OUT LOUD—LITERALLY GIVE YOURSELF A PEP TALK (CHECK YOUR AFFIRMATIONS ON PAGE 11!).
- ☐ RELAX IN A WARM BATH OR SHOWER.
- ☐ DO SOME MUNDANE CHORES.
- ☐ PLAY AN INSTRUMENT.
- ☐ CALL A FRIEND.
- ☐ IF YOU LIKE ORGANIZING, DO IT.
- ☐ CUT YOUR DAILY TO-DO LIST IN HALF, AND THEN CUT IT IN HALF AGAIN.
- ☐ STRETCH.
- ☐ WATER YOUR PLANTS (PLEASE DO THIS ANYWAY, REGARDLESS OF YOUR MENTAL STATE!).

WHAT ELSE HELPS YOU GO MICRO?

_____   _____

_____   _____

_____   _____

_____   _____

_____   _____

DREAMS AND GRIEF NIGHTMARES

A study by Dr. Joshua Black, a Canadian grief researcher whose work focuses on dreams and continuing bonds after loss, found it's common to dream of the deceased (human or pet) at least once after a loss.

Most people have negative dreams throughout life because life is stressful, and the stress can passively creep into our unconscious. Chances are you'll have more of them in grief because you're working through unresolved anger, guilt, and other complex feelings.

Don't be afraid of these dreams. Both the good and bad ones are reflective of your mind processing your grief and trauma while you're asleep. A good therapist will understand how bad dreams reflect your grief and what should be worked through in your sessions.

Rescripting: How to Reduce and Remove Power from Nightmares

It's not just that your trauma and grief affect your dreams; your dreams affect your trauma and grief process. Avoiding bedtime because of bad dreams? Not good. Instead of accepting a lifetime of crappy sleep, you have the power to try to turn a negative dream into a positive one. It's called *dream rescripting* and can decrease the chances of that nightmare returning. Neat, huh?

Trying it is simple. Once awake, change the details of the dream in one of two comforting ways:

1. Change the ending of your dream. For example, if someone is chasing you and you wake up out of breath, rewrite the script. Add a scene in which you stop running, turn around to see who's chasing you, and turns out it's someone or something you love in pursuit of an enormous hug.

2. Adjust the narrative by adding a sympathetic character at the beginning of your dream to help you to work through some of its challenges.

3. Rehearse this rescripted dream during the daytime for a week and see what happens.

What About Those "Good" Grief Dreams?

There are many reasons we'd want to dream about our person: to see them one more time, hear their voice, relive a memory, get a message from or give one to them. Some of these dreams are worth remembering because they're wistful and lovely and bittersweet. Perhaps you sit and giggle with your person or run around the park throwing water balloons at one another. Maybe you take a nap together or just hold each other while listening to music in the dark. Those are nice experiences to have, even if while unconscious.

So, what can you do if you haven't had one of these dreams yet? Dr. Black found that your dream recall rate is very important for you to "catch" one of these types of dreams. If you're someone who doesn't normally remember your dreams, it may be harder for you to remember these. You can increase your recall rate by starting to value your dreams. This can be done by writing them down or talking about them with others. (But just as you might want to increase your dream recall of a good dream, recording details of a bad one may also result in you having more of them, so consider avoiding that.)

YOUR DREAM JOURNAL

Name/date: _____

Draw it out:

What happened?

_____

_____

_____

How did you feel during the dream?

_____

_____

_____

What did you wake up feeling?

_____

_____

_____

Have you had this dream before?

_____

_____

_____

If you're waking up in the middle of the night and don't want to turn on
the light to write down a dream you want to remember, try quietly
recording a voice note on your phone.

Dream Incubation: Create Your Ideal Dream

Do you wish that you could have that perfect dream with your person? I do. Most of the dreams I had of my parents were limited to debilitating nightmares for the first couple of years (nobody told me about dream rescripting, not in a helpful handbook, not in therapy, not anywhere). And I found myself deeply yearning for glimpses of them in my sleep, wishing I could be dipping my toes into the languid, late summer waters of Lake George with my mom or hearing my dad's witty jokes once again. Turns out, just as you can reduce the charge of nightmares, you also have the power to train your mind to build dreams that can soothe you. Even if you're already having some positive dreams, there's always a narrative that you'd love to see play out.

Think through what your ideal dream would be like. Once you're finished—and this is the key—put some thought into it during those influential last moments before going to bed. Tell yourself how important this dream is to you and that you'd like to wake up after having it so that you can remember. If that's what your mind goes to bed with, there's an increased chance you might have some version of it.

I know this all may read a bit woo-woo, but I did, in fact, test this out for myself. And it worked. You never know.

Who is in it?

_____

Where does it take place? (One specific or general location or several?)

_____

_____

How do they look? What mood are they in?

_____

_____

What time of day is it?

_____

What else do you notice around you?

_____

_____

_____

_____

_____

_____

What exactly happens in the dream? Is anything spoken, or is it silent? What happens between the characters?

_____

_____

_____

_____

_____

_____

What do you feel at the end?

_____

_____

_____

_____

_____

What's the name of your dream?

_____

This is a great group exercise with family or friends all missing the same person. It's a creative way to see the different ways in which everyone wishes they could connect and share with the person you've lost.

Getting Through the Days:
Practices and Little Tricks

HERE ARE SOME exercises designed to sync up your mind and body in a restorative and healing way. These are designed to be deployed when you're unexpectedly taken aback by your grief (in a board meeting, on Zoom, in traffic, or on a date) and need some tools in your pocket to center and calm yourself, or when you have some precious alone time and want to use it wisely.

WAKE UP

I did promise I wouldn't insist that you practice gratitude all the time. But gratitude does help, even if you acknowledge it in bite-size doses. Many of us don't have five minutes of leisure time in the morning, but a lot of us have two. Choose somewhere you can sit comfortably and spend two minutes quietly thanking each part of your body for properly functioning. If there are parts that aren't working all that well, offer them kindness and hope that they will heal soon. Sometimes it's the tiny things that remind us that all is not lost.

I feel like this should go without saying, but please drink water! Our organs need it to properly function. You're likely to get more dehydrated when you're under stress. Studies have shown that being just half a liter dehydrated can increase your cortisol levels. Your heart rate rises, and you're breathing more heavily, so you're losing more fluid. Get yourself one of those weirdly large daily water intake bottles that are the size of your torso, and drink throughout the day.

BUTTERFLY HUGS

In the EMDR section of this book (page 77), I mention how therapists teach self-soothing practices to use both during and outside sessions. I love this self-administered bilateral stimulation (BLS) method. It's simple, comforting, and can be done anywhere (plus, it's a great tool to teach kids).

Sit with your back straight. Do some abdominal breathing; imagine there's a little balloon in your stomach that you slowly, smoothly, and deeply inflate and deflate.

Observe whatever is going through your mind and body.

Cross both arms over your chest so that your middle fingers are placed below your collarbone and the rest of your fingers are touching your upper chest.

Tap your shoulders gently with each hand, alternating hands between each tap, simulating the flapping wings of a butterfly.

Keep going until you feel more relaxed, observing whatever is going on in your mind and body, and make sure to breathe deeply throughout the entire exercise.

The butterfly hug was developed in 1998 by Lucina Artigas during her work with the survivors of Hurricane Pauline in Acapulco, Mexico, and has become standard practice for clinicians in the field working with survivors of man-made and natural catastrophes.

5-4-3-2-1 GROUNDING TECHNIQUE

This is a simple trick for managing anxiety. You know those moments when everything suddenly feels overwhelming? When the enormity of the loss of your person slams into you, you realize it's a forever thing, and you have no idea how you'll be able to move through it all? There are no magic solutions for grief, but there are tools. This technique has helped many of our community members. It's very grounding, which means it uses our senses to help us feel more attached to our surroundings and yank us out of the anxiety response.

5. **Look.** Name out loud five things you can see.
4. **Feel.** Pay attention to your body and say four things you can feel (the hair on the back of your neck, a soft pillow, the cold metal of a chair).
3. **Listen.** Identify three sounds (distant traffic, your stomach rumbling, birds tweeting), and say them out loud.
2. **Smell.** Say two things you can smell (your hair product, a meal in the oven, the garbage bin).
1. **Taste.** Name one thing you can taste (the onion from that bagel you had earlier, a trace of toothpaste . . . if you truly can't taste anything, name one thing you love to taste).

   Repeat if needed. (You can also do the exercises with five of each sense, then four, three . . .)

Yoga for Grief Support

THIS IS ONE OF MY favorite sessions offered to the Modern Loss community. It's led by Sandy Ayre, an occupational therapist and certified yoga instructor who has guided and soothed hundreds of our members worldwide from her Canadian base in Edmonton, Alberta.

Sandy and I started working together when the Covid-19 pandemic slammed into the world and sent us reeling through a new and unfamiliar terrain rife with fear, uncertainty, retriggered grief, and trauma. The overwhelming adjective we kept hearing from people: ungrounded. So, we started offering monthly virtual sessions to pull people together in their respective isolation.

Grief can leave us feeling disconnected from ourselves and the life we knew. When we are ungrounded, the mind can feel unfocused, the body can feel numb and dissipated, and the spirit can feel lost.

Being *ungrounded* is akin to feeling:

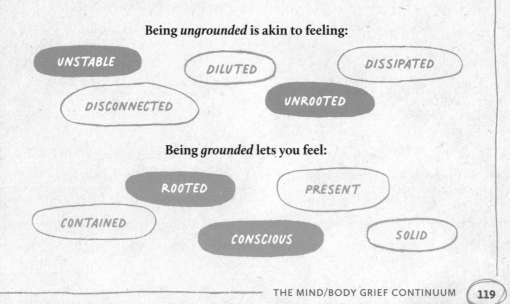

UNSTABLE   DILUTED   DISSIPATED

DISCONNECTED   UNROOTED

Being *grounded* lets you feel:

ROOTED   PRESENT

CONTAINED   CONSCIOUS   SOLID

The point of a yoga practice isn't to bypass your grief; rather, it's a way *into* your experience and gives you tools that promote loving and caring action toward yourself. You are fully present and conscious of what is happening in your body and mind in each moment, especially when those moments are emotional and challenging. Integrating loss requires acknowledging pain and depth and finding a way to recalibrate.

Here is a practice Sandy created to help gently bring you back into yourself. No need to be a seasoned yogi to do it. I'm certainly not.

● Supported Savasana ●

You will need either a rolled yoga mat or rolled blanket for under your back and another blanket or small pillow for your head.

Place the rolled blanket on the floor behind you. Sit on the floor at one end of the roll, and lay back so that it extends up your spine. Place a pillow under your head. Open your hands with palms facing the ceiling, and make sure your shoulders are moving away from your ears. Relax and let gravity gently stretch your chest. Your lower back should not be overly arched; if it is, move your hips away from the roll. Continue for ten to twenty breaths or as long as is comfortable.

What It Alleviates

One way the stress of grief manifests is in difficult breathing. The breath can be tight, constricted, or shallow. And the weight of grief often makes people hunch forward, rounding their shoulders as if they were curling around their heart. That position is understandable when considering the nature and vulnerability of grief, because it's a position of protection. It does, however, make it hard for the lungs to expand to take a deep breath. When you aren't breathing deeply and your body isn't getting enough oxygen, it can worsen feelings of worry, anxiety, and panic. This pose helps to facilitate deep breath, which can help activate the relaxation response. Stretching the chest and shoulders literally opens up the anatomy surrounding the heart and increases circulation. Bringing compassionate awareness to these areas is a powerful way to nourish the grieving heart. It is considered a gentle "heart opening" pose. How does laying in this position feel for you?

You may feel vulnerable with your heart facing upward and your body stretched open. Time to move on.

❁ Child's Pose ❁

From your supported Savasana position, bend your knees and roll onto one side. From there, press onto your hands and knees, then lower your hips onto your heels in child's pose. Reach your arms forward until your head rests on the floor (prop your forehead on a small pillow if needed). You can stretch your arms long to lengthen the back or let them rest heavy on the floor.

Now, your heart and the front of your body are protected and facing downward and your head is supported. This position can be very soothing, especially if you're feeling vulnerable. How do you feel in this position compared to the first pose? (There is no right or wrong in yoga. Simply notice which one feels more helpful to you in this moment.)

Try a variation now: Walk your hands to one side of the mat, so that your torso aligns with one thigh. This gives the opposite side of the body a deep stretch. Support your head with a pillow.

Taking a deep breath requires you to expand the rib cage in all directions. Compared to the first pose, where the focus was more on the front of the body, this variation makes it possible to feel the breath in the sides and back of the body. The more you can loosen the muscles of the rib cage, the more pliable the body will be as you breathe a deeper breath.

Hold each of these variations for five to ten breaths or as long as you're comfortable. Focus on where you feel the breath moving in your body: Can you feel the coolness of the air in your nose or the movement of your rib cage? Does your lower back rise and fall with the breath?

Deep, full, and effortless breathing is one of the simplest ways to ground yourself or center yourself in your own body. And it's a great way to turn on the relaxation response and calm the mind. By focusing on your breath, your mind thinks about one thing (how the breath feels moving in and out) versus everything (grief).

● Standing Forward Bend ●

From child's pose, press up onto your hands and knees, then come up to standing. For this next pose, you will need a chair, couch, bed, or table.

Standing in front of the chair, widen your feet to hip distance (or as wide as your yoga mat if you have tight legs or lower back), bend forward, and place your head and arms on the chair for support. Depending on the flexibility of your body, you may be able to use the seat, or you may need to use the back rest (or a higher surface). In this pose, your legs should take the weight of the pose so at any time you can lift your head easily.

Grief can be erratic. Your body may feel tired or physically drained and completely mentally unsettled. A paradox, but it's because the body and mind experience the stress of grief in different ways. Often the body wants to slow down, rest, be still. One can feel heavy

and slow to move, react, and respond. Yet the mind tries to figure out the un-figure-out-able, which makes it work harder to "fix" grief, resulting in disorganized thinking, anxiety, and difficulty concentrating.

This supported forward bend is very balancing for the body and mind. It invigorates and enlivens the legs (due to the stretch and strength needed to do the pose), and yet it calms the mind (supporting the head on the chair).

Hold for five to ten breaths, then slowly lift your head.

☉ Mountain Pose ☉

Mountain pose looks like regular standing, but from a yoga perspective, it's one of the most foundational and grounding poses of the practice.

Stand with your feet hip-width apart. Lift your toes off the floor, and press your feet into the floor. Find the point where the weight of your body is balanced between your heels and your toes. Next, make sure your knees are not locked. Slightly bend them in order to activate the thigh muscles. Stand up tall. Roll your shoulders back and down, and balance your head over them so that your earlobes align with your shoulders. (Notice if you are overly clenching in this pose. You want to feel sturdy and stable but still have an element of ease.)

Stand in mountain pose for five to ten deep breaths while you stay aware of the sensations in your body and your firm connection to the ground through your feet.

This pose is helpful for bringing awareness from outside yourself to your inner self. It's easier to navigate the unknown landscape of grief from a place of internal awareness, where you have a clear sense of your internal state, needs, and boundaries. Paying attention to the sturdiness of your legs can help create a sense of inner strength and perseverance. Notice the flow of your breath, and try to embody the qualities of a mountain and the breeze flowing over the slopes (breath): sturdy and easy.

Mountain pose is a great pose to use as a mini-break throughout the day.

Mindfulness

AH, "MINDFULNESS." Another one of those buzzwords that most of us probably couldn't easily define. So, what is it, actually? It's the state of being intensely aware of what you're sensing and feeling *in the moment*, without interpretation or judgment.

Modern Loss started offering monthly community mindfulness events when we went into Covid-19 lockdown and felt like we were losing our damn minds. The events were led by Annie Pearson, a certified mindful change coach and instructor. Her approach blends foundations of mindfulness and positive psychology to create effective methods of coping with stress and reducing anxiety, leading to increased focus, creativity, and resilience. I credit my ability to hang on to whatever shreds of sanity I had during those long months of isolation and fear to Annie's short, guided Zoom sessions.

Here are a couple of mindfulness practices to try. The first one was created just for you by Annie; it's a mind-body activity for releasing energy from emotions trapped inside the body—or, as my grandmom Sylvia would've called them, *shpilkes*.

BODY PART SHAKE-OUT

Stand or sit comfortably with your feet on the ground.

Move from one body part to the next, beginning with the feet and moving up toward the head. Move/shake/wiggle each body part while you repeat its name five times:

1. Wiggle your toes and say, "Toes, toes, toes, toes, toes."
2. Rotate your ankles and say, "Ankles, ankles, ankles, ankles, ankles."
3. Bend your knees and repeat, "Knees, knees, knees, knees, knees."
4. Shake your legs and repeat, "Legs, legs, legs, legs, legs."
5. Twist your torso at your waist and repeat, "Waist, waist, waist, waist, waist."
6. Wiggle your fingers and repeat, "Fingers, fingers, fingers, fingers, fingers."
7. Rotate your wrists and repeat, "Wrists, wrists, wrists, wrists, wrists."
8. Shake out your arms and repeat, "Arms, arms, arms, arms, arms."
9. Shrug your shoulders up and down and repeat, "Shoulders, shoulders, shoulders, shoulders, shoulders."
10. Gently move your head side to side and repeat, "Head, head, head, head, head."

TIPS:

🌀 Inhale and exhale deeply between each movement.

___

🌀 Listen to your body, and make any physical adjustments as needed.

___

🌀 It may help to use the same rhythmic pattern for each repeated word.

🌀 If you get up to your head and still have more energy to release, reverse the process, going from the head to the toes.

___

🌀 You can also complete the series with a final full-body movement while repeating, "Body, body, body, body, body."

How Does This Work?

Sometimes our mind-body-emotion can get stuck in a loop. Movement helps release the energy trapped in our bodies. Using the same technique as the body scan and labeling each body part helps the mind focus on something you know without question. There's no thinking involved except matching the name of the body part with the body part that is moving. The repetition of each word in a rhythmic pattern works as the connector between the body and mind, which helps to calm the overall nervous system.

ALTERNATE NOSTRIL BREATHING

Here's a calming breath practice for when you are feeling or thinking too much and want to ground yourself. I have done this in public and private. Do I look weird when doing it? Most likely. But I'll take looking weird for a minute over feeling like I'm going to spontaneously combust like the Spinal Tap drummer.

1. Place your index and middle fingers on the center of your forehead in the space just slightly above and between your eyes.
2. Your pinky (or ring finger) and thumb will come to either side of the nostrils.
3. Exhale completely.
4. On your next inhalation, close the **right** nostril by gently pressing your thumb against the skin side of your nose, and **inhale** deeply through the **left** nostril.
5. Release your thumb from your nose, close the **left** nostril by gently pressing your pinky or ring finger against the skin side of your **left** nostril, and **exhale** the **right** side.
6. Keep your fingers where they are and **inhale** through the **right** side.
7. Close the **right** nostril and **exhale** through the **left** nostril.
8. This is one cycle (**inhale** on the **left** side, **exhale** the **right** side. **Inhale** the **right** side, **exhale** the **left** side, always changing sides on the exhale).
9. Repeat the cycle for three to five minutes, or as long as feels comfortable to you. You may begin to feel the grounding effects immediately or within a few minutes.

TIPS:

🌀 Try closing your eyes to focus your attention on your breath.

🌀 Let your breath be smooth and controlled at a comfortable pace.

🌀 Aim for a long spine from your tailbone through the crown of your head (don't tuck your chin or tilt your head back).

🌀 As you get more comfortable, add a "hold" between breaths; for example, inhale for a count of five, hold for five, exhale for five . . .

How Does It Work?

This breath practice comes from the yogic tradition of *pranayama*, *prana* being energy. It is thought that breathing through the left nostril stimulates the right side of the brain (the part responsible for processing our emotions), and breathing through the right nostril stimulates the left side of the brain (the side that governs logic and thinking). Breathing through each side in turn balances the energy of both sides of the brain as well as both the sympathetic and parasympathetic nervous systems. This practice can help settle nervous energy, lower heart and respiratory rates, and improve your ability to think clearly.

Craniosacral Therapy

CRANIOSACRAL THERAPY (CST) is a light-touch, hands-on technique that releases tensions deep in the body to relieve pain and dysfunction and improve whole-body health and performance. Its practitioners believe the body has an innate ability to heal itself (sometimes referred to as the *inner physician).* CST involves facilitating or enhancing the body's natural capacity to heal when trauma or disease become overwhelming to the nervous system.

So much of grief feels like resisting what is real and holding on to the past by physically clenching our hands, jaws, and shoulders to the point where going about the day so tightly wound feels like your baseline.

I tried CST in the middle of the very long and torturous winter of 2020–2021, when I felt like society's and my own individual feelings of loss were piling up so quickly that they didn't have anywhere to go. So, I went to see Sally Washabaugh, who has worked as a craniosacral therapist and master-level energy practitioner at the Kripalu Center for Yoga and Health for more than twenty years.

Thirty minutes into the session, during which Sally very gently and subtly manipulated my body into different positions as I lay on a table, I felt calm, comfortably tired, and, weirdly, like different parts of my body were opening up after spending who knows how long in a state of tension. Since then, I have calmly breathed, napped, and gazed my way through these restorative sessions aimed at opening my energetic pathways. As Sally described it to me, when done right, CST helps to take off grief's edge and lets you relax and float on its waves as they ebb and flow.

In short, I still don't understand how it works, but for me it just does. My husband, who has also gone to her, loves to say that if she lived in a small village, she'd be the most important member of society. She's a true healer, and I really don't tend to speak that way. CST works so well for some but not for others. If you can find someone to help you as Sally helped me, you might feel a noticeable difference.

Even if you don't try CST, you can use a couple of neat tricks Sally taught me to quickly release built-up tension. I've done them while giving talks on Zoom, in waiting rooms, and while attempting to breathe deeply whenever my kids are driving me nuts.

Positional Therapy for Wrists, Hands, and Arms

Developed by neuromuscular therapist Lee Albert of the Kripalu Center for Yoga & Health

Relieve elbow and wrist pain/strengthen wrist extensors
Place a hairband or rubber band around your fingers. Exhale, press your fingers into the band, inhale, release. Continue for 30–60 seconds. Repeat several times per day.

Relieve tight hands/thumb
Squeeze the thumb into a palm like a taco; hold 60-90 seconds.

Sally added an effective twist on it, which comes in handy while you spend hours at your desk. Just press your fingers down directly onto any surface.

Relieve tight forearms
Stretch your wrist and palm; hold 60-90 seconds.

Seek Out Touch

TOUCH IS A BIOLOGICAL NEED. It's the first sense to develop in utero. It's integral to a newborn's emotional, mental, and physical well-being in those early stages of life and is important for humans in *all* stages. It has magical, scientifically proven powers in its ability to provide emotional release.

In our lonely grief, sometimes we desperately crave the tenderness of touch (remember all that physical isolation during Covid-19 quarantine?) and frequently with no commitment. I cannot encourage you enough to tap into this need. A little can go a long way.

Some ideas for getting yourself some healing contact:

● Get a regular manicure/ pedicure. Add the foot rub, warm clay wrap, and special salts, too.

● Book a massage (there are even therapists who specialize in grief massage).

● Get your hair cut/brushed/ blown out.

● Tell a trusted friend you need a big hug, a gentle squeeze, a hand on your back, a snuggle.

INTIMATE CONTACT

Grief may diminish or ramp up your sex drive. Sexual arousals and orgasms make us feel very much alive during a time when we are so focused on death. They also release feel-good neurotransmitters and pain-reducing hormones that can, at least temporarily, give us reprieve from the immeasurable pain or numbness.

Have sex. If you have a partner you're comfortable with, do it. If you're single, still do it . . . but be highly aware that you are in a sensitive place and try your best to choose wisely. Be sure to set and keep boundaries (and please practice safe sex, as unfortunately, STDs, STIs, and unwanted pregnancies do not respect grief). Find a friend or someone you trust to talk through what those might be and how to be held accountable to them.

Masturbate. This is an easy way to get some pleasure during a shitty time and can be a great alternative to having sex with the wrong person when you're so vulnerable. It can also help improve your mood and sleep. If you haven't done this a lot and need a bit of help getting started, several great apps offer guided self-touch sessions, such as Dipsea. Get yourself a decent vibrator and/or other sex toy and have at it. Don't be shy; it's just you with yourself!

Get Outside

"I've found that there is
always some beauty left —
in nature, sunshine, freedom,
in yourself; these can all
help you."

— Anne Frank

YOU PROBABLY SPEND most of your day staring at screens indoors. But our nervous systems are meant to interface with dynamic natural environments. We didn't evolve as a species inside a windowless galley kitchen or the Gap. Taking a forty-five-minute leisurely walk *in actual nature* lowers your stress, heart rate, and blood pressure and promotes sleep regulation.

Nature can be healing, but it's also raw, unfiltered truth. Spending time in the natural world exposes you to the timelessness of life, death, impermanence, and beauty in the world. The rich outside environment can help us connect with meaning and reality and abundance with loss—ideas that when you are cracked open by grief, you may be more in need of confronting than usual. If you spend time hiking, chances are you'll come upon a dead animal or a dead tree that is now giving life to other trees growing out of it. If it's winter, you'll be surrounded by the blanketed quiet of a snowscape, bare branches, and, hopefully, the reminder that they will bloom again. When you think about it, nature may be the most appropriate witness to our grief and the most logical setting in which we can sit with our losses.

Here are some of the benefits of nature-connected living, which, along with a healthy diet, exercise, and loving relationships with others, are vitally important for our overall well-being:

Wellness: Research shows that spending 120 minutes in nature correlates with statistically higher physical and psychological health.

Resilience: Living near green spaces in childhood has been shown to be a buffer against mental illness in adulthood.

Healing: Access to a window looking out on green spaces can have a beneficial outcome on surgery recovery and result in decreased use of pain medication.

Stress: Research shows that walks in pine forests can decrease heart rate and blood pressure, significantly lower cortisol levels, boost immunity, elevate moods, and improve sleep.

Attention: Attention restoration theory has shown that looking at green spaces helps us recover from attention fatigue and be more productive.

GREEN GAZING

Don't even try to tell me you don't have time to do this one. Do it while drinking your morning coffee or at any time of day when you're feeling fatigued from periods of prolonged focus and need your brain to recover from screentime overload.

1. Look out the window for five to ten minutes.
2. Allow your attention to wander over the landscape, enjoying anything you see that catches your attention. The gentler the movement, the

better. Some examples of natural manifestations that support *soft fascination* are the wind moving through the trees, flowing water, and the clouds in the sky. Cities have a lot of these things, too; let your eyes focus on anything natural, even if it's some plant boxes on a balcony.

SOUND MEDITATION AND FOREST BATH

You don't actually have to go *into a forest* for this, and, yes, you can and should be clothed, unless you love tick bites. Just go outside wherever is convenient: an open field, a garden, the beach. The important thing is to be outside in a place with some nature and to notice your surroundings through all your senses.

Find a comfortable place to sit. Close your eyes or soften your gaze. Tune into the sounds around you. Begin by noticing the ones nearby, then gradually focus on sounds coming from farther away. Stay with them for three to five minutes, then walk slowly as you take in the sights, sounds, smells, textures, and maybe even the flavors of your environment. When you feel ready, take some time to journal about your experience.

Right now I am noticing . . .

_____

_____

_____

_____

_____

_____

_____

_____

_____

_____

_____

_____

_____

_____

_____

_____

_____

_____

OUTSIDE GROUNDING EXERCISE

Walk slowly or stand on the grass barefoot. Notice how your feet feel as they connect to the ground. Breathe slowly and deeply as you notice how your body feels connecting to the earth.

Special thanks to Micah Mortali, the founder of the Kripalu School of Mindful Outdoor Leadership in Stockbridge, Massachusetts, for advising and contributing to this section.

A Note on Joy, Humor, Laughter, Celebration, and the Guilt You Shouldn't Feel About Any of It

THE GRAVESIDE SCENE was somber at the funeral of my college friend David's[2] grandmother. Nearly everyone was in black, murmuring condolences to each other on the death of the family matriarch. The rabbi chanted the *Kel Maleh Rachamim* (Jewish Prayer of Mercy) in soft monotone. Even the weather was bleak, and not even a slice of sunshine breaking through the slate-gray skies.

A few minutes after the casket was lowered into the ground, there was a gust of wind. The tree branches creaked and swayed deeply. The dead leaves rustled around the headstones. And the purple suede *kippah* that Cousin Stevie was wearing was blown off his head; up into the air it flew, swirling around a few times, before promptly landing smack on the wooden coffin that had just thudded onto the earth several feet below.

Everyone alternated between staring down at the hole and staring at each other, not knowing what to do. Nobody dared say anything. After all, it was a funeral, and there was a corpse lying right in front of everyone. Suddenly, an

[2] Name has been changed to protect anonymity.

exasperated Cousin Stevie loudly exclaimed in his thick Baltimorese accent, "*Daaaaamnnn* . . . that was real leather!" There was an immediate communal exhale as everyone melted into laughter and acknowledged that even Grandma Doris[3] would have deeply appreciated such comic timing.

We don't shy away from humor in life. Why? Because life's messiness is full of absurdity. So, why should we shy away from humor in grief? If life is messy, by extension so is death. Grief is an extreme feeling: crying until you can't breathe. Humor can be an extreme feeling: laughing until you can't breathe. They are not unrelated. The phrase "Laugh or die" exists for a reason.

Dear reader, I am certainly not directing you to laugh during a funeral (although if you do, know that it's okay). There will be moments in loss that offer absolutely zero potential for humor, and you will know what they are. Also, it's okay if you don't think you're ready to laugh and feel a bit of lightness—although I really hope that some of the contents of this book have already foiled that plan. But what I *am* telling you is to not feel any guilt about the moments that suddenly do provide humor, joy, and lightness. Do not feel bad or ambivalent about celebrating good things that happen, be it a raise or a marriage or a new child or just a decent Tuesday. It doesn't make you disrespectful of your grief or of your person's death. It makes you human. And alive. Which is nice because you are both.

So go ahead, make the "dead person" jokes. Dissolve into hysterics when the DJ plays "The Lady Is a Tramp" at your saintly mom's wake in a wonderfully misguided effort to fulfill her request for Sinatra tunes. Enjoy the confusion of the guy at the hardware store who sees you buying a shovel and

---

[3] Name has been changed to protect anonymity.

answer, "I already did that!" after he jokingly asks, "Are you gonna go bury your husband?"[4] Let yourself say, "He's dead to me, yeah," when some unsuspecting soul quips that you must no longer have anything to do with your former fiancé after you share that he took you to a sports bar on your birthday.[5] Embrace the fine art of gallows and societally inappropriate humor.

And I beg of you, do not give a flying fig about what other people think. Feel no guilt when you find yourself actually having fun and not thinking about your person. You'll still grieve and feel like absolute crap, I promise. You still love your person as much as you always did. But during a time in which very little makes sense, a reminder of your humanity, of your quirky parts that appreciate the ludicrous elements of this mess, can bring levity to an otherwise dark place. Lean into it with all you have.

Did you know there's an Association for Applied and Therapeutic Humor? Isn't that neat? Their studies show that 39 percent of people felt a decrease in stress *simply anticipating humor*. Laughter can lower cortisol levels and increase the production of dopamine, endorphins, T-cells, and immune proteins. So the next time you even think about feeling guilty for cracking a "dead mom" joke, remember that you're actually taking care of yourself by doing so. Your dead mom would probably want that.

Keep a running list of the stuff that's making you laugh, the activities that bring you joy, and the lighter moments that unexpectedly arise:

---

[4] And then assure him it's totally fine when he feels ABSOLUTELY AWFUL afterward—no need to be mean, here!
[5] These are all real-life examples from the Modern Loss community. Best crew ever.

Grief Island, Grief City

EXTERNALIZING GRIEF as a place that can change and be reanimated with time can help us recognize our own transformations.

Here is a wonderful exercise created by Emily Rapp Black, the aforementioned genius of a friend and writer.

Whenever we run Modern Loss retreats together, Emily guides the group through the following exercise she created, and I am always amazed at the variety of tableaus people share.

> **First, imagine the early period of your grief is an island. Look at it from a distance and describe your island in detail.**

What is its landscape?

_____

_____

_____

What's the weather like?

_____

_____

_____

Who is allowed to visit? Who isn't?

_____

_____

_____

Draw it out using any materials you like.

**Now, change gears completely and imagine
your current grief as a city. Look at it up close.**

Who would be there?

_____

_____

_____

_____

_____

What are people doing?

_____

_____

_____

_____

_____

What are the buildings like?

_____

_____

_____

_____

_____

As our grief changes, so does its landscape. Sometimes grief is thorny, dark, and rocky. Sometimes the memories that create the corridors of our loss are also a relief and refuge. What about your grief is sometimes a comfort? What parts of your city and island may also offer pockets of relief and surprise?

_____

_____

_____

Draw it out using any materials you like.

"There are the people who will show up at your funeral and the ones who will show up on a Thursday. Find the ones who will show up on a Thursday. TUESDAY WORKS, TOO."
— Catie Lazarus
(writer and comedian)

Navigating
(And Negotiating)
Friendship and
Social Dynamics

POSSIBILITIES AND PITFALLS

How Our Relationships Shift In Loss

PROFOUND LOSS is one of the biggest fires we can pass through, and we are forged within it. In other words, loss changes everything about you: your routine, your future plans, your outlook, your world. And when we go through an intense and shaping experience, we will inevitably grow apart from some members of our circles. When that fire dies down, relationships with some people in your life may not look or feel the way they used to.

Why is there an entire section dedicated to friendship and social dynamics in this book? Because, for some reason, there's not a lot of attention specifically paid to this topic in most discussions about grief. There are plenty of public conversations and resources about supporting parents left behind, helping children through grief, adjusting to life after losing a partner, managing the financial and other estate headaches after a death, coming to terms with anger, or reimagining life without the people you expected to share it with. But it's weird that there isn't a lot of public acknowledgment and expectation of one of the most common secondary losses coming out of grief: the loss of or drastic shift in friendships. Friendship is a powerful, sacred bond, and it, like all others, is tested by the force of grief.

Here is the good news: Chances are great that there are people in your life willing to perform the simple, difficult act of showing up and acknowledging whatever it is you need to have acknowledged. After my mom died, a bunch of different friends from various parts of my life who barely knew each other started talking to each other during the shiva. Most of them had no idea what to do for me and how to do it, given their own busy lives, where they were managing their own issues, but they wanted to figure out ways to at least make sure someone was checking on me. Suddenly, an email chain was born that assigned a different person to call weekly and offer to join me as I binge-watched *Grey's Anatomy* or endlessly wandered through the Strand bookstore or Central Park. After the first couple of months, they started making monthly Sunday brunch reservations around New York City so that I'd be forced to show up for in-person support over eggs and unlimited Bloody Marys. As insipid as "brunch plans" may seem, that one monthly guarantee was sometimes the thing I hung my sanity on.

Eventually, that same brunch club realized I needed a break from crying all over Manhattan and might need to cry somewhere more bucolic, so they took me to one of their homes in the Berkshires for a weekend of hiking, bourbon, and crying in a location with lower population density. Some were college and grad school friends, some were work friends, some were forever friends, and some were made-in-New York friends. But this show of support put them solidly in a new category: the friends who had my back, no matter what emotional state I was in.

Some more good news: I truly believe your social support system has endless growth possibilities after a loss. You'll probably make new friends who you never would have made otherwise and who will support you in ways you never imagined you needed until they provided it. There will be unexpectedly kind gestures, like the PA on my friend Katie's film who sent her a beautiful message with a quote from Proust that she actually ended up reading at her mom's memorial. There will be people who come out of the woodwork after hearing about your loss because they know what it feels like to need someone to sit with them in the mess of it all (and not someone to swoop in with hollow platitudes, unsolicited advice, false assurances, or ridiculous comparisons). There will be complete strangers you meet at cocktail parties or while sharing niceties while you keep an eye on your kids at the playground who turn into meaningful parts of your life when you both realize you've gone through hell.

There will even be people with whom you may not have otherwise crossed paths. After Gabi's father and stepmother were killed in a home invasion, she found support among those whose loved ones had also been murdered. This unique support group gathered biweekly in a church basement in Harlem, and its members connected over violent losses that everyone else in their lives wanted to avoid mentioning.

YOUR FRIENDS AFTER LOSS

(Hint: You'll probably grow your circle more than you'll shrink it.)

THE ONES WHO STAYED IN YOUR LIFE

THE ONES WHO COME INTO IT AFTERWARD

But now, some not-great news that you might as well read here: You will probably lose some friends. And I sure as hell wish someone would have told me all of this when I needed to hear it.

The truth is, for one reason or another (and mostly the reasons are about them, not you), not everyone can deal with your unfiltered loss. People you assumed were your "ride-or-dies" will inexplicably disappear or suddenly look incredibly awkward or interested in examining their fading manicure, or obsessively check their phones when you're in their orbit. A lot of very well-meaning people will unintentionally say or do dumb shit. Some examples: "I miss the *old* you," or "Are you ever going to get over this?" Others will seem like they're doing their absolute best to make you feel invisible and invalidated. They might pretend that the person you lost never existed.

To add insult to injury, it's nearly impossible to predict which of your friends will fall into which category. As if you don't have enough going on already.

These realities may bring a certain level of additional pain to your life. When you're grieving a loss, what you long for—and what you deserve—is for everyone to be open to you sharing with them, however brutal or sad that story might be.

After my mom's car accident, what hurt the most was silence, or an inability by others to acknowledge what had happened. It was also painful to have caring people in my circle—from coworkers to forever friends—reach out with the intention of helping but then never following through or putting it on me to tell them exactly how I wanted their help. I had no idea what to tell these people in the moment. (Word to the wise: "If there's ever anything I can do . . ." rarely helps someone, unless your goal is to have them blankly stare at you while trying not to blurt out, "Yeah, can you bring my person back from the dead?") Very few asked if I needed something specific, so it was difficult to know what to ask for. And then the conversation was just . . . over. I didn't have the energy to figure out a better reply, so a lot of people simply faded away.

It's hard and hurtful. It suuuuuuucks. And there's often no way around the work of rebuilding your support system.

I do believe some people genuinely want to be better at supporting others who are navigating the hellish grief maze, but a lot of times it takes a helping hand from the one going through it. I believe that a lot of friends who screw up while trying to offer support deserve a chance—or four—to get it right, if not in the short term, then after you take a break from them. It may not be fair (and when has the word *fair* ever played into grief?), but the reality is that it's on us grieflings to figure out how to express our needs and requests to those who would love to provide meaningful support. It's easy to be hard on others when you're full of sadness and fury and anger. But a lot of them deserve a chance for you to help them help you; after all, it's not their fault our society sucks at this.

And, finally, remember: You have agency. Grief opens you up in ways that are raw and powerful and scary, to be sure, but also in ways that allow for deeper, more satisfying connections with people. Connections that are anchored in trust, vulnerability, and empathy. My friend Amanda Clayman once wrote a piece entitled "Age 40: Ain't Nobody Got Time for That." It was about how, when she hit that milestone year, she realized her time was too precious to waste on frivolous connections. After my parents' deaths, suddenly I craved quality in friendship far more than quantity. Grief: Ain't Nobody Got Time for That.

The following pages will guide you in thinking through a lot of this. It's helpful to take an active role in building your support system by considering who in your life you can count on (or how to find those people), what you need, and how to ask for it. It's also helpful—and important—to figure out how to create your own boundaries in friendships, like how you can respond when someone says literally the worst thing ever or how to decide when a relationship no longer serves you in a positive way. Remember, nobody emerges from this unscathed, so you need to find the people who are willing to be forged in this fire alongside you.

The great paradox of grief is that even as the world closes around you, it can simultaneously open. It may not happen as fast as you want it to, but trust me, there are more ride-or-dies out there if you're willing to let them in.

BE KIND, BEREAVED ON BOARD

(If only we could navigate the world with this on our backs)

"There's the kind of support you ask for and the kind of support you don't ask for. And then there's the kind THAT JUST SHOWS UP."

-Carrie Bradshaw at Miranda's mother's funeral, Sex and the City "My Motherboard, Myself" (s4, E8)

Grief scares people. You know the friends you've known forever who you assume will show up when things are at their worst? Sadly, this isn't always the case. It can feel like a betrayal, and as cliché as this sounds, it truly is *not* about you. Grief brings up complicated feelings for everyone, and sometimes people don't know what to say, they say the totally wrong thing or, even worse, they say nothing at all. This doesn't mean you're a bad person or they're bad people; it means that grief is hard. You would rather not deal with it, right? So, some people who have a choice in the matter (at least for now) just decide not to deal.

But there will be new people entering your life who will feel immediately like forever friends. Someone you met for a day a few years ago could reach out and show up. You might meet someone through grief groups or the Modern Loss community that you can't imagine *not* knowing. These new "ride-or-dies" will be just that. Why? Because they came to you in the most turbulent space. They sat in the tornado with you, and they're here to stay.

That may not seem true when you're being ghosted by a close friend when you *really* need to talk to someone, but trust me: It *will* happen (and I am speaking from personal experience).

For so long, I was terribly nervous to talk about my grief out loud. What would people think of me? What if I wasn't grieving the "right way"? (And what does that even mean? Turns out it means nothing! There is no test to ace, no boxes to check.) What if I broke down into inconsolable tears and the person got uncomfortable, unsure how to help me? What if people saw my vulnerability as a character flaw? But when I started talking, it felt like an enormous emotional exhale, like some of the stress and built-up sadness were relieved in some way by the act of sharing it. My confidence in sharing my story—and my needs—grew, and the more I continued sharing my story (and hearing others' stories, too), the more I met people who I wish I'd met in any other way but now can't imagine living without. What I have learned is that even though grief is a hugely personal experience, we are not islands. If Covid-19 has taught us one thing, it's that we are connected to each other in ways we never knew.

WAYS IN WHICH GRIEF CAN IMPACT FRIENDSHIPS

1. A friend might get confused by your inability to participate in the friendship in the way that you used to and even assume you just want to be left alone. They were used to the old you . . . the one who something didn't suddenly (or slowly) happen to. You might be a bit angrier or quieter now, and this will shift the way in which you interact with one another.

2. You may feel exhausted hanging out in social settings when all you can do is feel sad and grief stricken. You may feel like you're watching people from afar, like watching fish inside a tank, and there's nothing worse than feeling alone in a group of people.

3. It may be hard for friends to relate to your experience if they haven't personally gone through something remotely related to what you're feeling or managing (or failing at feeling or managing). Worse, they might make one-to-one comparisons like "My pet died last week, so I know how you feel." Or they might try to distance themselves from your experience. "I don't know how you do it," or "I can't imagine how you're coping" only emphasizes how hard grief is and is hardly a pep talk.

4. It's a litmus test for who's in your corner and who isn't when things get hard. You'll be both hurt and surprised by the people who do and don't show up. But the people who show up now will likely *always* show up, and there's a great deal of comfort in that.

5. If you lost a friend, other friends might be on completely different paths in terms of their grief and expect you to feel like they do when they do. That's not realistic. Tension can erupt when you're not aligned in your anger, okay-ness, or nostalgia. You might find yourself in icky conversations about who's missing the friend most. That's a game nobody wants to win anyway, but it's a common experience.

6. In this death-phobic culture, we're great at avoiding the fact of our mortality. Our suffering may remind others of how close they could be to something happening to them. Some people will fall out of your life—and occasionally not even realize they're doing it—simply because you remind them of a truth that terrifies them: Everybody dies.

7. Your priorities might change at least in the short term. You might want to spend more of your nonworking time with family, with a therapist, or taking care of your health. Everyone needs to come to terms with the fact that there are only so many things you can do and with so many people in a day. Even Beyoncé.

The People in Your Life and How They Matter

I PROMISED MYSELF I wouldn't quote too many dead white men in this book but admittedly I've been impressed by the ancient wisdom of Aristotle. To be clear, the guy was kind of awful in major ways—like when he defended slavery and opposed the notion of human equality—but was onto something powerful when he classified friendship into three different categories: utility, pleasure, and of the good (guess which one is the hardest to find but also the most meaningful?). Keep these in mind along your grief journey, as they all play important roles:

Friendships of utility: These are the talented professionals/healers who help you in concrete, particular ways: the therapists, body workers, doctors, and anyone you pay to assist you. Also possible on this list: hairstylists, bartenders, the yoga teacher who gives you space to sit on your mat and weep throughout class.

Friendships of pleasure: These are the happy disruptors: friends who make you laugh, ply you with cocktails, take you dancing, invite you to karaoke even though your voice is horrible, text you funny messages and NSFW videos to be sure you giggle at least once a day.

Friendships of the good: These are the faithful friends who feel like family (hopefully without the dysfunction). The people with whom you can share your secret self, including your darkest, angriest thoughts (*Why my mom and not my coworker's?; I hate everyone; What is the point of life?*), and who will not judge. Instead, they acknowledge, support, and help you find a way to move past that thought or feeling (and if they can't, they'll book an appointment with a therapist and take you to the office). They'll send you food, love notes, packages, and will never forget to check in. When you call them and say you need help, they'll ask, "What can I do?" and if you don't know the answer, they'll suggest a few things and then do them.

ARIGATA-MEIWAKU (ありがた一迷惑): THE STRUGGLE IS REAL

It's clear the English language doesn't have the right words to capture the complicated and messy feelings of grief, while those brilliant Germans have come up with *kummerspeck*, which literally means "grief bacon" and alludes to the excess fat gained by emotional eating. Please meet another one I love: *arigata-meiwaku*. It's the Japanese term for an act someone does for you that you didn't want them to do and may have actually even tried to avoid having them do, but they went ahead with it anyway, determined to do you a favor, and then things went wrong and caused you a lot of trouble, yet social conventions required you to express gratitude for all of it (long explanation due to the fact that, again, there's just no term for this in English).

When it comes to grieving, I personally interpret this as the work that frequently falls on the *griever* to do the heavy lifting and make others feel more comfortable in their discomfort. For example: "I've arranged a memorial brunch you didn't ask for, and I need you to give me a list of names and pay for the invitations and also the printer needs all of this by 5 p.m.," or "Here's some food that you can't eat, but if I don't get a thank-you note after a week, I'll get passive aggressive and not continue to reach out to you." Please know, you're not the only one who feels this way.

Build Your Bullpen

NO SINGLE PERSON can fulfill all your grieving needs—not even a romantic partner or best friend. But if you carefully think through the strengths of the people in your life, you may find your go-tos. In my experience, it's better to identify them in advance and on a rolling basis rather than try to figure out who to call when in a moment of crisis at 1:42 p.m. on Christmas Eve. And if they aren't there, go out and find them. They need you as much as you need them.

Who appreciates good storytelling, for when you need to share some memories?

_____

Who in your life makes you laugh, for when you need some levity?

_____

Who in your life is super organized, for when you have shit to arrange (estate, belongings, or just help with cleaning the kitchen you've ignored for weeks)?

_____

Who's good and trustworthy with kids and can take them off your hands when in a scheduling bind or when you just need to mentally decompress or go on a walk and weep for a bit?

_____

Who's your adventure buddy and down for spontaneous escapes? (Doesn't matter if they can't be trusted with much other than that!)

_____

Who's empathic and emotionally available to hold space for your grief?

_____

Who doesn't have a lot of family/social responsibilities and might be able to easily visit—and even sleep over to make sure you're not alone?

_____

Who's a doer and can organize group plans on your behalf in advance of a trigger day, or just a Sunday morning?

_____

Who's a hugger? (I'm not joking. The need for physical comfort is very real sometimes.)

_____

Who always has a creative solution to a problem that feels unsolvable? Maybe you need guidance in setting boundaries with coworkers or family members. Or someone to help you sell your person's car.

_____

Who could you ask for a loan if you're in serious financial straits? (Note: This is only for when you really need to pull the emergency lever. I strongly caution against mixing friendship and funds. Another idea: Consider who might be willing to start a crowd-funding campaign for your needs.)

_____

Now, go to them when you need it.
Extra credit if you reach out now and ask if you can have them on call.

REMEMBER . . .

As long as you aren't hurting yourself or anyone else, you have permission to:

- Let people know when they're not being helpful and why
- Not act *at all* in the way your friends and social circles would like for you to act
- Tell them when it feels like they are actively trying to make you feel like crap (I don't believe this happens frequently, but it happens)
- Be upset when people don't respect your boundaries and abilities
- Not spend too much time trying to be kind and considerate about other people's discomfort around your grief

"TO FEEL IS TO BE VULNERABLE. To believe vulnerability is weakness is to believe that feeling is weakness. To foreclose on our emotional life out of a fear that the costs will be too high is to walk away from the very thing that gives purpose and meaning to living."

—Brené Brown, Daring Greatly

Give People a Chance to Understand

IT'S PAINFUL TO WAIT for friends to perfectly intuit our pain. We might resent them when they can't automatically support us in the way we need. But there are several reasons someone may not be properly coming through for you. They could be silently grieving something themselves, feel helpless or upset that you're upset, or would rather deny hard things out of habit. It's worth trying to express your needs and what you're going through. Grief has already made you vulnerable, and the seemingly worst has already happened. What's one more act of vulnerability?

If you could describe what grief feels like to someone who hasn't experienced it yet, how would you do that in an effort to give them a chance to connect with you? Write it here, and try to communicate that to them.

_____

_____

_____

_____

_____

_____

_____

_____

_____

_____

When my mom died, I kept telling friends I wished I could briefly insert a microchip into their brains so that they could understand what I was feeling. Maybe we'll be there in a few years, but for now, here's a little empathy trick I learned from expert Kelsey Crowe, PhD., that can help people put themselves in your shoes. Ask them about the worst thing they've gone through and how it made them feel. They might appreciate being shown how to help. In my experience, most people really want to, and it's worth giving them the chance to get it right before writing them off entirely.

> "I am figuring out which parts of my personality are mine and which ones I created to please you."
>
> — Lora Mathis, "The Dust on this Poem Could Choke You."

Figure Out Your New Boundaries, Then Set Them

I SAW A GREAT MEME RECENTLY. It was a photo of Oprah delighting her audience with one of her surprise giveaways. But instead of "You get a car, and you get a car, and you get a car!" the block meme font screamed, "You get a boundary, and you get a boundary, and you get a boundary!"

If only I'd had the self-awareness and self-confidence to lay down and stick to my own boundaries in those earlier days of grief—both in general and specific to various people and areas of my life—I'd probably have noticed a world of difference. As it happened, trying to take control within a tornado wasn't giving me a big sense of routine, control, or peace. Instead, I experienced only chaos, which worsened my grief.

Embrace my favorite emoji/text combo, the perfect combination of rejection and care:

NO. 🩶

Setting boundaries now might help enable you to hold on to some of the friendships and family relationships that otherwise might suffer in the short and long term, which of course causes further suffering, and that's not what you need right now. Try not to think of boundaries as an offensive move but rather a defensive one that helps you to protect yourself in a vulnerable state, be it for a few minutes or months on end. They will change over time, even from one day to the next, so adjust accordingly.

Here are some ways to do so:

◉ **Limit** who can see your posts online. Not everyone deserves to witness your feed, especially if you're feeling vulnerable or if people post rude or insensitive comments.

◐ **Choose** wisely who you let into your bubble. Be cautious of those who are suddenly love-bombing you with best friend vibes before they've spent any time with you at all.

◑ **Be kind but firm.** "No" is a complete sentence that will serve you well. If someone suggests an activity they're hoping might help you, but it doesn't resonate (marathon training, basket weaving,

pub crawling, whatever), it's okay to simply say "no." (It's always nice to add that you appreciate their thoughtfulness.)

◐ **Don't be afraid** to tell someone you're not able to be present for them in the way you might normally be. You cannot pour from an empty cup. If they say you're being a bad friend, don't believe them. It's okay to let them go, at least for now.

◑ **When all else fails,** stop responding. You already get all the credit in the world for multitasking grief and even just brushing your teeth some days.

And a few more . . . come up with
your own here so that you have
them at the ready:

_____

_____

_____   _____

_____   _____

_____   _____

ENFORCING YOUR BOUNDARIES

I'm a proponent of maintaining friendships whenever they can be saved
and strengthened. But don't hold on to one that consistently hurts. Only
you know your boundaries. Figure out what they are, and if it comes
down to it, stop allowing people into your life who cross them. Here
are a few situations that might fit the bill—it might be time to cut ties if
a "friend":

- Uses your vulnerability against
you

_____

- Does not support you

_____

- Does not respect things you say
in confidence

- Continually breaks promises

_____

- Insults, puts down, or humiliates
you

_____

- Says you're too sensitive or
shames you

If Someone Is Being Cruel or Abusive in Social Interactions:

- Hold them accountable. Call them out.

- Recognize when someone is gaslighting you. Some people have a special talent for rewriting the narrative (I didn't mean it like that; you're just interpreting it wrong.)

- End it. Remove their access to you. You have absolutely no obligation to leave the door open to anyone who hurts you. You've been through enough.

How to Recognize Toxic Positivity

KNOW THE PEOPLE WHO want you to feel "good vibes only! 🙏"? Those are the toxic positivity police, and you should steer clear of them. There are no wrong emotions. You are doing hard things and should never be ashamed to have whatever day you are having. Beware of variations of the following:

- You just need to try harder.

- Tough things will only make you stronger.

- No excuses!

- You're overreacting.

- Try to look on the bright side!

- Stop making a hard situation even harder on yourself.

- Don't be so negative!

- No challenge, no change!

Self-love is awesome, and not all positivity is toxic. But forcing someone to feel positive all the time, without validating how stressful and complex situations can be, ends up slamming shut the space to talk. Toxic positivity steamrolls a griever's feelings, telling them how they *should* feel and that they're to blame if they can't see the positive in the situation. **Try to gravitate toward the people who say variations of the following:**

- It's cool; all feelings are valid.

- It's okay to rest when you need to.

- I'm listening, and that sounds really hard.

- How can I support you?

- That's awful. I hate this for you.

- I'm full of rage on your behalf. This is unfair and hard, and I'm here for you.

SAD LIBS

Practice some exchanges that might feel uncomfortable to imagine. They're nice to have in your back pocket when the need arises.

I'm feeling _____ right now, so it may take me a while
        ADJECTIVE

to _____ , but I really appreciate you
    RESPOND TO YOUR TEXT, RETURN YOUR PHONE CALL, ETC

reaching out.

I'm feeling _____ , so I don't have the energy to
        ADJECTIVE

_____ right now, but I'll be in touch as soon as I can.
    VERB

When you said/wrote/texted _____ to me, it really

made me feel _____ .
        ADJECTIVE

Thank you. I didn't realize you sent me a _____ on

_____ . I didn't see it and haven't been checking social
    FILL IN SOCIAL MEDIA PLATFORM

media that much lately. Would love to hear from you via text or email for right

now; it means a lot to me.

I'm sorry you're having a hard time with _____ ,
                    TOUGH SITUATION

and I'd like to be there for you, but I'm dealing with _____

_____ right now and feeling overwhelmed.
    TOUGH SITUATION

It meant a lot that you asked me to _____ . I can't
                    ACTIVITY

this time, but I'd really appreciate if you'd ask me again. I might be up for it

another time.

THE 10 PEOPLE YOU MEET IN HELL

Originally published on Modern Loss by Erin Donovan

———— ✆ ————

Here is a brief introduction to the kinds of people you're bound to encounter in your darkest moments.

1. **Competitors at the Sad Olympics:** No matter what has happened to you, something *so much worse* has happened to them! Or to someone they know, or to someone they heard about, or to someone they scrolled by once on Facebook.
   - "I knew her better than you did."
   - "We were better friends, so my grief is more painful."
   - "You're not, like, an actual orphan."
   - "At least you got to say good-bye."
   - "At least you didn't have to say good-bye."
   - "You got an inheritance, though."
   - "Right, but you knew it was coming . . .?"

2. **The Feelings Police:** The ones who will try to make you feel like a terrible person if you're doing anything other than shopping for black veils or throwing yourself onto a coffin. No one gets to tell you whether you're grieving "correctly." You're allowed to not cry when you don't feel like crying. You're allowed to feel everything. You're allowed to feel nothing. You're allowed to take a minute and not think about death at all.

3. **Dismissers and Minimizers:** Incapable of emotional intimacy or sitting in discomfort, they will try to shoehorn you back into "being normal" as quickly as possible. There is no platitude too empty or dumb for these folks. These verbal acts serve only to get the speaker past their own feelings of powerlessness. People can be uncomfortable for two minutes and not die. It's really not a big deal.

   - "Time heals all wounds!"
   - "God doesn't give you more than you can handle."
   - "When a door closes, a window opens."

4. **The "Well, At Least!" Brigade:** Any statement that starts with this does not need to be said aloud. Ever. Just no. This applies to every context and every situation—every single crappy human experience that has ever or will ever exist. Don't say it. But definitely not when someone has just experienced a major loss.

   Empathy is not a finite resource. My only response to people who "remind" me there are starving children around the globe is "You don't seem like you're doing much for them, either."

5. **Vultures:** Another empathy-impaired sect who love to glom onto anyone else's tragedy to perform their own, completely fake, humanity. These will be the people you barely know who are so aggrieved for you. At first you might think, "Oh no, maybe they lost someone in a similar way." But upon further conversation, you realize . . . no, they're just Blanche DuBois'ing all over you.

   These are the people keeping Nancy Grace in business. They love spectacle and celebrity tragedy and the weight of the entire world in tiny, bite-size increments. If you're feeling charitable, you might say to yourself, "Here is a person living in a constant state of fear and anxiety who needs new information that meets them at the level their brain is already operating at."

6. **Ennoblers:** The ones who want to put you on a pedestal (or lock you in a suffocating glass box) and talk over you whenever things get too messy. They will use words like "brave" and "grace" while shushing you. Seen frequently around horrific acts of violence. (Why do so many reporters ask someone who recently had a loved one murdered if they forgive the killer? Who is that for? Who is that serving?) You don't need to behave for anyone.

7. **The Paying Audience:** These people show up and expect you to Perform! Your! Sadness! They will ask insanely probing questions, or they want the really grisly details of your loved one's death. They seem to have some sick need to watch you fall apart.

8. **Happy Fools, aka the "Huh, Did Something Happen?"**
   Contingent: Nothing in this world that has happened to someone else could even approach how interesting their lives are. Sometimes  these people can be nice to be around (for short periods) because you can temporarily forget anything bad has happened to you. But long-term exposure to people this self-obsessed might wind up making you feel isolated or that your pain isn't serious.

Luckily, the cure for these people is simple. The nanosecond you mention that you need to talk about what you're going through, they will vanish. No conflict necessary.

9. **Hallmark Baby Birds:** They love to dispense glib inanity in times of crisis. Not nearly as invasive as some of the aforementioned types, but it's like they've only learned how to relate to other human beings via greeting cards and fortune cookies.

Example: I've had so many random people tell me that "my mother would be so proud of me for how I've handled all this." Three things: (1) Do I know you? (2) There's just no way that's true. Look at how mean I'm being! My mom would put soap in my grown mouth if she saw any of this! (3) My mom is a pile of ashes; I don't think she's actually feeling anything these days.

10. **The "Weren't You Not Even That Close?" Truthers:** It hurts because it's true, but that's not the point. When someone dies, you're not just grieving all the good times, you're grieving for the inability to make

things better. You're grieving all the things you meant to say, all the questions you meant to ask, and all the things you meant to apologize for that are now just frozen in the amber of being sort of crappy.

Remember What Helped

WHENEVER I INTERVIEW someone for the Modern Loss newsletter, I always end by asking them to share the most helpful thing someone did in their grief.

For *CONAN* writer Laurie Kilmartin, it was the "My mom died of Covid 4 fucking days ago, wear a fucking mask!" masks that her best friend ordered from Etsy. For Cynthia Nixon, it was the friends who came through *after* the initial grief circus died down and made it clear they were bearing her in mind. For comedian Alyssa Limperis, it was her enormous Greek family pushing its way into her home the minute her father died (turns out the "overstepping" was just what she needed). For stylist Stacy London, it was the friend who left a plush robe, fuzzy slippers, and chocolate bars at her apartment with the note "These will just feel good."

For poet Saeed Jones, it was the friend who turned up at his new Harlem apartment after his mom died, automatically started unpacking boxes, ordered a burger, and, when it arrived without ketchup, called the restaurant and said, "My friend's mom died and he hasn't been eating and I finally got him to eat and it didn't come with ketchup. Get some over here!" If that sounds silly, the effect was enormous: It made him laugh, showed him that there were still people in his life who were fighting for him, and reminded him that he could fight for himself, too.

For me, it was my friend Justin, a classmate from the Columbia Journalism School deadline trenches. Upon learning of my mom's car accident, he sent the following email:

> **Subject: bullshit**
>
> Rebecca, I just heard about your mom. She was amazing and always made me smile and always had a smile on her face. This is total fucking bullshit. I am pissed!!!! Love, Justin

And though I was appreciative of the hundreds of other emails I received that week, his was the only one I remember in detail. He was willing to sit with me in all my fury and disbelief and shock and make it clear that I wasn't alone in having extreme emotions.

As you can see, the answers are different, but they all have the one thing in common: clear recollections of who provided support and how. From the ridiculous and over the top to the more poignant and practical, people will say and do amazing things for you in your loss because people can be awesome.

It helped me to keep a running list of these, not only because it was nice to remember loving acts but it also served as ideas for how I could better support others in the future. I suggest you do the same.

Who said/did it?   What was it?

_____   _____

How did it make me feel?

_____

Who said/did it?   What was it?

_____   _____

How did it make me feel?

_____

— —

Who said/did it?   What was it?

_____   _____

How did it make me feel?

_____

— —

Who said/did it?   What was it?

_____   _____

How did it make me feel?

_____

If you ran out of room here, that's terrific! Start a separate log in the back of the book or elsewhere.

Real and Imagined Bullshit You Might Hear

SOME MAY SEEM EXTREME, but these are all comments that have been made to members of the Modern Loss community, including myself, and I'd wager that a version of one of these has been said to every person who's experienced death loss. Because we are still grief illiterate in our culture, and some people are, honestly, dolts. It's unfair that we have to be the ones to educate others, but someone's gotta do it. Think about what you might say if/when someone lobs one of these insensitive, hurtful "reassurances" your way.

Take a crack at responding to any that might apply to you. Here, I'll go first:

> ### "I APPRECIATE MY MOM SO MUCH MORE NOW."

What I really want to say: *Oh wow, I am SO thrilled that my excruciating, violent loss of a person who will never meet my children and who was one of the two people on Earth who loved me unconditionally served as a helpful growth opportunity for you. Thanks for completely bypassing my pain and turning my loss into a catalyst for your gratitude. See you in hell! xo!*

What I probably will say: I'm happy that you have your mom in your life and that you have a great relationship. But when you say that, it's hurtful and emphasizes my loss. I'm sure you didn't mean for this to land the wrong way and that it came from a good place. So, I'm sharing this not to make you feel bad but so that you don't repeat this to someone later in the same way in which you probably wouldn't tell an alcoholic how grateful you are that you have no long-term issues from regularly pounding Goldschläger in undergrad.

AT LEAST YOU ALREADY HAVE A HEALTHY CHILD / CHILDREN.

What you might really want to say: *Do you have more than one child? Do you feel like losing one of them would not be such a big deal since you have the other one? I guess what you're saying is that my child wasn't special enough to be missed, and I can just fill that horrifying, gaping hole in my heart with a person who wasn't him or her, and I should be grateful. If you lose one of your children in the future, be sure to give me a call so I can remind you that you have another one and you should just get on with it and it's no big deal because children are interchangeable, by your logic. Also, fuck off.*

What you might consider saying instead: My child is not replaceable. It's not okay to say that to me.

I HONESTLY WOULDN'T SURVIVE WHAT YOU'RE GOING THROUGH.

What you really want to say:

_____

_____

_____

_____

What you might consider saying instead:

_____

_____

_____

_____

I HEAR THAT'S THE WORST WAY TO DIE.

What you really want to say:

_____

_____

_____

_____

What you might consider saying instead:

_____

_____

_____

_____

YOU KNOW WHAT
YOU SHOULD DO . . .

What you really want to say:

_____

_____

_____

_____

What you might consider saying instead:

_____

_____

_____

_____

> THEY'RE IN A BETTER PLACE / GOD NEEDED THEM MORE THAN WE DID.

What you really want to say:

_____

_____

_____

_____

What you might consider saying instead:

_____

_____

_____

_____

> YOU CAN ALWAYS GET PREGNANT AGAIN.

What you really want to say:

_____

_____

_____

_____

What you might consider saying instead:

_____

_____

_____

_____

I KNOW YOU DON'T WANT TO HEAR THIS, BUT ...

What you really want to say:

_____

_____

_____

_____

What you might consider saying instead:

_____

_____

_____

_____

YOU'VE LOST ALL OF YOUR JOY /
I MISS THE "OLD" YOU.

What you really want to say:

_____

_____

_____

_____

What you might consider saying instead:

_____

_____

_____

_____

YOU'RE SO YOUNG; I'M SURE YOU'LL MEET SOMEONE ELSE!

What you really want to say:

_____

_____

_____

_____

What you might consider saying instead:

_____

_____

_____

_____

BUT DIDN'T YOU NOT
HAVE A GREAT
RELATIONSHIP WITH THEM?

What you really want to say:

_____

_____

_____

_____

What you might consider saying instead:

_____

_____

_____

_____

What you really want to say:

_____

_____

_____

_____

What you might consider saying instead:

_____

_____

_____

_____

BUT THEY DIED SEVEN YEARS AGO...

What you really want to say:

_____

_____

_____

_____

What you might consider saying instead:

_____

_____

_____

_____

> WAS HE WEARING A SEATBELT / SICK / USING DRUGS /
> ANY OTHER INAPPROPRIATE REQUEST FOR DETAILS??

What you really want to say:

_____

_____

_____

_____

What you might consider saying instead:

_____

_____

_____

_____

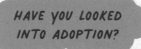

HAVE YOU LOOKED INTO ADOPTION?

What you really want to say:

_____

_____

_____

_____

What you might consider saying instead:

_____

_____

_____

_____

YOU KNOW THEY WOULD WANT YOU TO BE HAPPY.

What you really want to say:

_____

_____

_____

_____

What you might consider saying instead:

_____

_____

_____

_____

> LET ME KNOW IF YOU NEED ANYTHING!
> (OFFERED FOR THE SEVENTH TIME
> WITH NO SPECIFICS ATTACHED.)

What you really want to say:

_____

_____

_____

_____

What you might consider saying instead:

_____

_____

_____

_____

WHEN YOU'RE AT A LOSS FOR
HOW ELSE TO RESPOND:

Thanks for sharing! ☺

My mom, Shelby, was the most wonderful person I knew. That doesn't mean she didn't have her quirks, though! And one of them was how the excess of human love and care she had for the people important to her occasionally spilled out in the form of well-intentioned suggestions. She constantly worried about my uncle Steve, her only (and fully functioning, mind you) brother: about his health, his happiness, his ability to safely parallel park. This was the woman who would regularly snail-mail me articles with the important parts highlighted in yellow *and* circled with a Sharpie, so you can imagine how she occasionally got on Steve's nerves. He told me that whenever my mom's recommendations got to be too much, in an effort to both respond kindly to her good intentions and nip it in the bud, he'd offer a warm smile and a "Thanks for sharing, Shel!" (Internal translation: *Love you mean it but fuck off!*)

So whenever you're at a loss for how to respond—or aren't in a position to be completely honest—a simple "thanks for sharing!" with a smile will do the trick. In your mind, you know exactly what you're really telling them. I'll thank Uncle Steve on your behalf.

Why do you ask?

People just *loooooooove* to gossip and have for thousands of years. Humans needed something that would help them keep up to date with friends and family as they spread out across distances, and networks of *Homo sapiens* were becoming too large for everyone to effectively groom everyone else. In other words, we actually *evolved* to gossip. But just because we have an inherent need to know all the salacious details about what went down in a certain situation, it doesn't mean we have an obligation to share them.

If you don't feel like honestly responding to something wildly inappropriate like "Was she wearing a seatbelt?" (yep, some people do this when I tell them my mom died in a car accident), or "Was he sick?" or "Did you get genetic testing before becoming pregnant?" please consider grinding the conversation to a halt by—this is key—*kindly and innocently* offering these four simple words: *Why do you ask?* (You get a bonus point for slightly tilting your head to the side like a parakeet.) Because, really, *why the hell are they asking?* If they can't give you a reasonable response (IMHO nothing less than "Because my own personal fate is inextricably tied to your response"), then my hunch is that you will be met with uncomfortable silence and perhaps an unintelligible bumbling excuse, and you will have successfully permanently ended that exchange, thank you very much.

Dating

THIS TOPIC WARRANTS AN entirely separate book, but it is a major social interaction you may have after loss and worth addressing here. The bottom line: Dating is different now. It could be due to a romantic relationship that ended because they died or how your person's long illness, traumatic death, or inability to be born affected you. You're different now that you are living in "The After" of loss. So, your needs are probably different, too.

Here are some things to consider:

What exactly *are* your needs? Do you want someone who will take charge more? Be more nurturing? Allow you to set the tone and plans for when you see each other?

❂ ❂ ❂

Keep an open mind. You may think you have a very specific type, but it may have changed. If someone eagerly asks you out who seems great but who you have a general-but-not-necessarily-overt interest in because they don't seem to fit your "type," there is nothing wrong with giving it a try. Kind of like the wedding gown I thought looked a bit weird on the hanger: It could end up fitting a lot better than you assume.

❂ ❂ ❂

Ask for setups. Sure, hit up Bumble. But also reach out to friends, family, and other trusted people who know you *and* what you're going through, and ask them to set you up on some thoughtfully matched blind dates.

Decide what to share. Death and grief are icky topics to many, but you shouldn't feel like you can't talk about your loss. Consider if you can handle dating someone who can't handle your reality. If you can't, please do not date them.

❧ ❧ ❧

Proceed with caution. We all screw up in the dating experience, even without grief folded in. We have the tendency to screw up even more when we're raw and feeling particularly needy of love. Dating while grieving *must* fill your needs. You may be extremely selfish, which also may mean that you have very little to actually give back to someone else for the time being, and the other person will have to be truly okay with that.

CERTIFICATE OF APPRECIATION

Bestowed upon

ME

for just getting through the damn day.

Signed

_____

(and Ryan Gosling, because he'd probably also be very proud of you)

CERTIFICATE OF APPRECIATION

Bestowed upon

_____

FRIEND WHO HAS BEEN AWESOME

for _____ .

Signed

_____

(and Harry Styles, because he'd probably also be very proud of you)

"Feelings, and feelings, and feelings.
Let me try thinking instead."

— C. S. Lewis, A Grief Observed

Returning to and Getting through Work

WHEN BEREAVEMENT LEAVE RUNS OUT
(OR NEVER EXISTED IN THE FIRST PLACE)

The "Take Your Grief to Work" Days

SO. The funeral's over, all you want to do is fly as far away as possible or stay in bed, but you need a paycheck so you can afford life. It's hard enough to go back to the office after a week at the beach, so it can't be surprising that returning to work after a death can be a rough ride. On top of the fact that you might get very few vacation days, job expectations have risen, boundaries between work and home life have blurred more than ever (Slack chats from the bedroom, anyone?), and it's hard to be functional, effective, and anything but miserable and stressed at work (times infinity) when you're grieving a loss. You may also be expected to be physically present every day if you work somewhere like a grocery store, hospital, or school.

Be realistic about your options and capacity to work. Maybe you can shift to flextime; maybe you can take some paid leave (or unpaid leave if that's possible for you). Your boss or supervisor will likely *not* bring this issue up with you because, sadly, in our culture, we are often looked at as having unlimited capacity. But your capacity will be less, or it will look and feel different. That's normal.

You also might lose yourself in work you love (or hate) and in a job you love (or hate, or love/hate) in a way you haven't before. You also might *expect* this to happen and find that it doesn't. You won't know until you know.

- Email Tasks
- Cry
- Prep Presentation
- Zone Out
- Department meeting
- Look at old photos

The bottom line: You *will* bring your grief to work with you, and some days it'll be easier to focus than others. This remains the truth for a long time and even if you aren't dealing with an immediate loss, you could probably stand to have your professional life work a little better for your evolving needs.

Consider Your Work Needs
(Knowing They Might Shift)

IN AN IDEAL WORLD, as Tré Miller-Rodriguez pointed out in her Modern Loss piece "Game Planning Your Grief," employee orientation would cover more than work safety and sexual harassment; it would also include grief education. Trained counselors would explain how to interpret the body language and conversation cues of the bereaved and offer ideas for supporting a grieving colleague. Yet most employers aren't prepared to manage grief—not just the initial stages when an employee returns to the office but also the stress and anxiety and diminished productivity that can come of it when it's not well supported. In reality, it's on the mourners to relearn how to perform, interact, and care about the reports and quotas and KPIs that simply no longer qualify as emergencies to us.

With that in mind, think through some things that might serve you well, knowing that these may change over time. Keep coming back to this list, and see if you'd like to ask HR/your supervisor about the following:

- Do you need to work from home?

- Is it possible to start out part-time for a couple of weeks so that you have ample downtime to transition back? Or start out by taking three-day weekends so that you're able to ease back in? (When my dad died, I requested a couple of two-week periods of unpaid leave to take a few months after his death; the time period I thought I'd need to give myself some care and also deal with estate matters.)

👁 Would you like a flex work schedule so that you can do grief counseling or other important sessions that can't take place outside of business hours?

👁 Are you in a performative job like education? If so, can you ask for a period of time during which you can reduce your course load/office hours and take on more committee or background work? Your job may be quite different, but if you don't ask for what you need (which means identifying what you need or trying to), then nobody else will give it to you.

👁 Would you benefit from a period of time that isn't officially considered in performance targets/employee evaluations?

HOW GRIEF CAN AFFECT PRODUCTIVITY

👁 Grief brain is real. You will probably have concentration and memory issues. Schedule and take breaks.

👁 You may feel kind of useless at work for a while. Sometimes, just going through the motions is enough of a step.

👁 Your peak productivity hours might feel like they've changed. If that happens, try to adjust your schedule (take breaks at different times, consider arriving and leaving early, etc.).

Find Your Point Person

IT CAN BE HELPFUL to have some attention deflected during the first several months after your return to work. We spend so much time at our jobs that it's worth making the setting as comfortable as possible. Unless you want to share your story and needs with your entire group of colleagues (exhausting), I suggest identifying a point person you can give updates to. It doesn't have to be your BFF. It just needs to be someone type A-ish and compassionate and who people can go to when they want to ask *literally anything* about you for a period of time, including what might be helpful to send your way, how involved you may be able to be on a certain project, and your scheduling availability. This can be either a supervisor or coworker who might be able to help with the following:

- Sending short emails informing people about your situation (with details approved by you) and how they can specifically offer help.

- Upon your return, sharing your favorite treats or food, and asking colleagues to take turns leaving a small token of care on your desk (no note or visit required).

- Letting people know that you're not in the mindset to talk about your loss at the moment and to please steer clear from asking questions. (Tip: You can tell them a simple "Nice to see you" is easier than "How are you doing?")

- Asking coworkers not to play the sad trombone as soon as you walk into the room, avoid looks of pity, fall silent, or completely ignore your loss—whatever you need (or really *don't* need).

womp womp

Make a list of who might make a good point person and what you might ask them to do.

_____

_____

_____

_____

_____

_____

_____

_____

_____

_____

_____

_____

_____

_____

_____

_____

_____

_____

QUICK NOTE ON MAKING RASH DECISIONS

A few days after you come back to work, you may have a strong desire to stride into the office, Jerry Maguire–style, and loudly announce your resignation, then head out with the company fire-tailed Peruvian beauty fish in a Ziploc bag. But as good as that might feel in the actual moment, many therapists strongly suggest allowing yourself to wait six months to a year before making any significant life changes that are informed by your new worldview. Grief can be the catalyst for meaningful shifts, including career changes. But if you're seriously considering a big move, please consult a therapist before ditching your paycheck and flying to Bali.

Helpful Tips to Consider,
Courtesy of the Modern Loss Community:

FOR YOU ALONE:

❦ Change your routine just enough so that it doesn't feel like everything is exactly the same as it was pre-loss.

❦ Take *all the breaks* available to you. Does your employer have a "wellness room" or one dedicated to pumping/nursing? Anything that has a lock where you can be alone or something as far away as possible from most of your other colleagues? Calendar some daily time (multiple times, if needed) where you can sit for some quiet time, even if you don't think you need it. It'll be easier to get through the rest of the day.

❦ If you feel absentminded and nervous to miss a big deadline, meeting, or just complete your daily to-do list, use every scheduling and reminder tool in your kit—sticky notes, alarms, calendar notes, tell a friend to check in, and whatever other methods you can employ.

❦ Carve out space to just breathe. Memories may stage sneak attacks that feel like a punch in the gut. Come undone when you need to, and know when and how you need to step away. Do whatever you need to center yourself (and use some of the helpful exercises in the Mind/Body section on page 99).

❦ Think about how you can create a bridge period between your work schedule and the next part of your day. Can you listen to a calming song while you walk home or watch a funny video in your home office before descending into the dinner-time chaos?

WITH OTHERS AT WORK:

◉ Suggest outdoor/walking meetings. They feel better than sitting in a conference room.

◉ Ask colleagues you enjoy to invite you out for lunch or coffee once a week. You can always decline but will know another invitation is coming later.

◉ Speak openly with colleagues from time to time, when you're ready. It will encourage people not to walk on eggshells around you.

◉ Figure out your response to "I'm sorry for your loss," because *you will hear it a lot.* (Hint: A simple "thank you" suffices.) For more on this, see the section on friendship and other social interactions, on page 147.

◉ Request time off or flex/WFH time during milestone dates. You know exactly when those are, so plan well in advance, and you can always change your mind.

◉ Give a heads-up to your manager or your trusted person if you do decide to work on one of those trigger days so they can support you (or at least stay the hell out of your way).

Of course, this is a lot harder if you're a freelancer or in another role where you work with multiple projects or clients. If this is you, be honest with clients and realistic with setting expectations and committing to deadlines.

GRIEF DAY OFF

Need a personal day to feel griefy? Need to unplug and recharge? Require a break from making any decisions whatsoever but still need ideas for how to spend the time in a way that nourishes your need to connect with your loss? Here's a trusty guide to making the most out of your grief day off (henceforth known as GDO). Choose one from each section that appeals to you, and your plans are made. It's the ultimate self-care activity sans decision-making pressure. #GDO

Eat

- Your favorite childhood cereal
- Açai bowl (for when you want to feel healthy-ish)
- Any comforting soup (matzah ball, ramen, Samgye-tang, and so on)
- Pizza and/or pasta
- Trader Joe's dark chocolate peanut butter cups
- All the cheese
- Nacho Cheese Doritos® Locos Tacos Supreme®
- Ben and Jerry's Americone Dream®
- Wagyu burger with regular *and* sweet potato fries

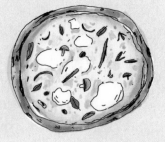

Wear

- Velour
- Something with glitter
- Nothing but your finest skivvies
- Fuzzy slippers
- Sweats
- Anything of your person's
- Whatever your interpretation of "black tie optional" might be

---

Watch

- *Fleabag*
- *The Office*
- *Wandavision*
- *August: Osage County*
- The entirety of the Harry Potter series
- *Dead to Me*
- *The Notebook*
- *Departures*
- *Coco*
- *Steel Magnolias*
- *Beaches*
- *Philadelphia*
- *The Breakfast Club*, or any John Hughes movie
- *Never Have I Ever*
- *John Wick* (It's about a widower!)

Listen

- *Tidal* by Fiona Apple
- *Carrie & Lowell* by Sufjan Stevens
- *It's All Right to Cry* from Free to Be . . . You and Me
- "Everybody Hurts" by R.E.M.

Keep Me In Your Heart by Warren Zevon

Wake Me Up When September Ends by Green Day

"It's Quiet Uptown" from *Hamilton*

Literally anything by Juan Gabriel

The Bodyguard soundtrack

Any Celine Dion ballad from a movie where somebody died

The Ballad Collection by Boyz II Men

Do

Go to a float tank and cry.

Sit in a closet and cry.

Buy yourself some nice toilet paper—the quadruple-ply kind that you could sleep on—to cry into.

Just stay in bed. (Remember thinking like a crab? No need to push yourself beyond your abilities.)

Load on your least waterproof mascara, have a good sob, and take artsy photos of your face.

Go to Starbucks and tell them you need the fanciest and most indulgent drink to kick off your #GDO, and then explain what that is. They might even throw in a muffin.

Cue up a song you know all the words to, roll down your car windows, and let it rip.

Visit puppies and kittens at your local shelter.

Book a spa appointment for a treatment you've never heard of before.

Be the Workplace Change You Want to See

LET ME START OFF by saying that you **do not** have to turn your grief into a mission, so this section may not apply to you at all. But given the abysmal state of bereavement protections in the United States and several other countries around the world, if you are indeed motivated to make things better for the next person policy-wise, you may have the power to get your employer to prioritize and promote empathy in the workplace as they never have before. At the time of this writing, there is no national policy, and in theory, if your company has no policy, you could technically be fired for not coming to work the day after a death.

As time goes by and you (hopefully) feel less controlled by your grief, you may want to think about how your experience might serve to usher in some positive culture change and potentially create a ripple effect for other colleagues who will have a better experience when they're faced with loss. Remember that this book is also meant to help you build resilience and grow post-trauma, so don't hate me for including this suggestion!

Some ideas:

◉ Work with your employer to create a return-to-work resource kit for those returning from bereavement leave.

◉ Advocate for the addition of "mental health days" as floating holidays.

◉ Ask HR to consider appointing "empathy agents," compassionate employees who can let management know when someone seems to be struggling.

◉ If you work at a consumer-facing company, insist on customer emails that allow them to opt out of communications around triggering holidays or using more inclusive language. (I'm absolutely loving the Mother's Day and Father's Day opt-out trend!)

⦾ Ask leadership to acknowledge hard parts about "exciting" holidays, both actual ones and those of the Hallmark ilk.

⦾ Leave a favorite grief book on your desk and see if it catches anyone's eye.

⦾ Consider starting an employee grief group with rotating speakers, or host monthly happy hours for other grievers at a local bar.

Your Grief Manifesto

OH, FRIEND. You didn't think I'd leave you hanging at the end of this book with no takeaways, did you? Before you look up and rejoin this overwhelming world, take a moment to read these tenets and rights you are due along the long arc of your loss. And when you don't have time to flip through this book to find a particular line to get you through the day, just turn to this one (and keep a picture of it on your phone) to remind yourself what you deserve every damn day.

I HAVE THE RIGHT TO MAINTAIN BOUNDARIES AND PERSONAL SPACE.

I HAVE THE RIGHT TO BE TREATED WITH RESPECT IN MY GRIEF.

IT IS NOT MY JOB TO MAKE OTHERS FEEL COMFORTABLE ABOUT MY LOSS.

I WILL SPEAK UP OR ACT WHEN SOMEONE OR SOMETHING IS MAKING ME UNCOMFORTABLE.

I WILL DO MY BEST TO NAVIGATE SURVIVAL MODE SO I CAN FIND MY WAY BACK TO THRIVING MODE.

I WILL NOT ADHERE TO OTHERS'
TIMELINES AND EXPECTATIONS ABOUT
WHEN I SHOULD BE "OVER" MY GRIEF.

I WILL COMMIT TO SHARING MY
STORY IN WHICHEVER WAY FEELS
MOST COMFORTABLE TO ME.

I WILL SEEK OUT HELP (HOWEVER I CHOOSE TO
DEFINE THAT) WHEN I NEED IT.

WHEN I'M HAVING A HARD GRIEF DAY, I
WILL BE COMPASSIONATE WITH MYSELF
AND DO MY BEST TO DO SELF-CARE
(HOWEVER I CHOOSE TO DEFINE THAT).

AS LONG AS I'M NOT HURTING MYSELF
OR ANYONE ELSE, I'LL DO GRIEF HOWEVER
I PLEASE, THANK YOU VERY MUCH.

Add anything else to your personal grief manifesto (and feel free to fill it in along the way):

_____

_____

_____

_____

_____

_____

_____

_____

_____

_____

_____

_____

_____

_____

_____

_____

_____

_____

_____

_____

Notes

Some extra space to continue any exercises from earlier in the book, or just write down whatever comes to mind whenever you need to.

_____

_____

_____

_____

_____

_____

_____

_____

_____

_____

_____

_____

_____

_____

_____

_____

_____

Acknowledgments

THANK YOU.

To my friend, unofficial editor, and program coleader, Emily Rapp Black: You are proof that some of the strongest bonds can be formed in adulthood. Thank you for reading both the 2 p.m. drafts and 2 a.m. drafts, and somehow sending them all back within fifteen minutes with the perfect feedback.

To my longtime agent, Rebecca Gradinger, and Christy Fletcher from Fletcher & Company: You listened to my dreams for this book and made them come true smack in the middle of a pandemic.

To my editor at Running Press, Jess Riordan: You were a pleasure to work with after coming to this project months down the line while we both juggled Covid-19 WFH with small children and primarily communicated during hours when most people should be sleeping. And also to Jennifer Kasius, the longtime Running Press editorial director who immediately understood my vision for this project; Jenna McBride for your artistic vision; and Elizabeth Graeber for your beautiful illustrations. You are a dream team.

To the generous practitioners who consulted on, guided me through, and contributed to this book. Your intelligence, expertise, and empathy were priceless in my writing and research:

Pria Alpern, PhD, of Center Psychology Group in New York City

Sandy Ayre, occupational therapist and certified yoga practitioner of Yoga for Grief Support (yogaforgriefsupport.com)

Anne D. Bartolucci, PhD, CBSM, of Atlanta Insomnia and Behavioral Health Services

Joshua Black, PhD, grief dream researcher and host of the *Grief Dreams* podcast (griefdreams.ca)

RoseAnna Cyr, MA, MT-BC, LMHC

Millet Israeli, JD, LMSW

Micah Mortali, MA, founder of the Kripalu School of Mindful Outdoor Leadership

Annie Pearson, mindfulness expert and founder of Empowered Purpose (empowered-purpose.com)

Larry Smith, SMITHMag and Six-Word Memoirs

Sally Washabaugh, craniosacral therapist

Dan Wolfson, PsyD, of Experience Camps and in private practice in NYC

Brennan Wood (executive director) and Alysha Lacey (program director), The Dougy Center

To Ivan Nascimento and Vanessa Guerrero, who provided brilliant graphic design support along the way: *Los quiero, mis panas.*

To my favorite group text members and three of the most creative, supportive and hilarious humans I know: Tim Federle, Benj Pasek, and Shaina Taub. Can't wait to be inspired by all that you do next.

To my friends around the country, who continually checked in on my sanity, checked in on my work, and just checked in: Rachel Axler, Kerry Donahue, Leslie Gray Streeter, Katie Rich, and Rachel Reichblum Rosenzweig.

To my Modern Loss cofounder and friend, Gabi Birkner: You have one of the kindest hearts—and sharpest editing skills—I have ever known.

To Arden Brown, Shelby Layton, and Sammy Watson, the magical child caregivers who allowed me to continue my professional life throughout the uncertainty and fear of Covid-19 in 2020 and 2021.

To Glynnis MacNicol, doyenne of modern New York City and my favorite sunset dining partner.

To Ruth Ann Harnisch, Jenny Raymond, and the Awesome Foundation: You always have the tough love and the belief in me that I sometimes forget I have in myself.

To my Spring 2021 college intern, Estee Rosenberg, who brought me such joy, camaraderie, and creative brainstorming sessions during a time of such sadness and solitude.

To the ones I've loved since I was Rebecca Rosenberg.

To my mom, Shelby Rosenberg, and my dad, Ray Rosenberg: I will always wish you were here instead of this book.

To my little boys, Noah and Elliot: You have taught me so much through your own empathy and resilience and you make me laugh out loud every single day. I do this work in part to teach you how much love, understanding and all-around good can come out of sharing our stories. I adore you.

To my husband, Justin: Thank you for understanding the importance of the conversation around grief, for appreciating its ability to color everything, for never shying away from it over the course of all these years, and for enabling so many mini writing retreats by taking the kids on a Target run when a chapter had to get finished.

I write the following earnestly: A special thank-you to those who gave me side-eye, commented how depressing working with grief sounded, and generally doubted that anyone would gravitate toward an endeavor to pull people together surrounding loss and storytelling with humanity and laughter and hope. The fact that you did so only further convinced me that a white space needed to be filled to normalize the conversation and that we needed a platform for everyone who "gets it" to fly their flags, and make this universal topic something that didn't necessitate side-eye. You only propelled me forward in building exactly what I have always known this project to be: life affirming.

Resources

A diverse list of some of my favorite grief resources. Noted accordingly when associated with a certain community or tradition, and many of these books pertain to multiple categories.

Books

ALL THE GRIEF THINGS

Grief Works: Stories of Life, Death and Surviving by Julia Samuel

Grieving While Black: An Antiracist Take on Oppression and Sorrow by Breeshia Wade

H is for Hawk by Helen Macdonald

It's Ok That You're Not Ok: Meeting Grief and Loss in a Culture That Doesn't Understand by Megan Devine

Modern Loss: Candid Conversation About Grief. Beginners Welcome. by Rebecca Soffer and Gabrielle Birkner

ANTICIPATORY GRIEF/TERMINAL ILLNESS

The Bright Hour by Nina Riggs

When Breath Becomes Air by Paul Kalanithi

FINDING MEANING, RESILIENCE, AND POST-TRAUMATIC GROWTH

The AfterGrief: Finding Your Way Along the Long Arc of Loss by Hope Edelman

Anxiety: The Missing Stage of Grief by Claire Bidwell Smith

The Beauty of What Remains: How Our Greatest Fear Becomes Our Greatest Gift by Steve Leder (Judaism)

Keep Moving: Notes on Loss, Creativity, and Change by Maggie Smith

MISCARRIAGE/STILLBIRTH/CHILD LOSS

Miscarriage: A Memoir, a Movement by Jessica Zucker

Notes for the Everlost by Kate Inglis

The Still Point of the Turning World by Emily Rapp Black

PARENTAL LOSS

The Adult Orphan Club by Flora Baker

The Art of Death by Edwidge Danticat (BIPOC)

Can't We Talk About Something More Pleasant? by Roz Chast

Crying in H Mart by Michelle Zauner (AAPI)

Dancing at the Pity Party by Tyler Feder

The Dead Mom's Club by Kate Spencer

Everybody Died, So I Got a Dog by Emily Dean

How We Fight for Our Lives by Saeed Jones (BIPOC & LGBTQ+)

Life's Accessories by Rachel Levy Lesser

The Long Goodbye by Megan O'Rourke

My Dead Parents by Anya Yurchyshyn

Notes on Grief by Chimamanda Ngozi Adichie (BIPOC)

OBIT by Victoria Chang (AAPI)

SIBLING LOSS

The Art of Losing It: A Memoir of Grief and Addiction by Rosemary Keevil

The Empty Room: Understanding Sibling Loss by Elizabeth DeVita-Raeburn

I Had a Brother Once: A Poem, A Memoir by Adam Mansbach

Men We Reaped: A Memoir by Jesmyn Ward (BIPOC)

Untwine: A Novel by Edwidge Dandicat (BIPOC)

PARENTS OF BEREAVED CHILDREN

A Parent's Guide to Raising Grieving Children: Rebuilding Your Family after the Death of a Loved One by Phyllis R. Silverman and Madelyn Kelly

PARTNER LOSS

Black Widow by Leslie Gray Streeter (BIPOC)

From Scratch by Tembi Locke (BIPOC)

Ghost Rider: Travels on the Healing Road by Neil Peart

The Group by Donald L. Rosenstein and Justin M. Yopp

Hot Young Widows Club by Nora McInerny

My Wife Said You Might Want to Marry Me by Jason B. Rosenthal

Splitting the Difference by Tré Miller Rodriguez

The Year of Magical Thinking by Joan Didion

PET LOSS

P.S. I Love You More Than Tuna by Sarah Chauncey

When Dogs Heal: Powerful Stories of People Living with HIV and the Dogs That Saved Them by Jesse Freidin, Christina Garofalo, Dr. Robert Garofalo, and Zach Stafford (LGBTQ+)

PRACTICAL AND TACTICAL

Everyday Resilience: A Practical Guide to Build Inner Strength and Weather Life's Challenges by Gail Gazelle, MD

Rewilding: Meditations, Practices and Skills for Awakening in Nature by Micah Mortali

Tapping In: A Step-by-Step Guide to Activating Your Healing Resources Through Bilateral Stimulation by Laurel Parnell Ph.D.

What Matters Most: The Get Your Sh*t Together Guide to Wills, Money, Insurance and Life's "What-ifs." by Chanel Reynolds

THE SCIENCE OF GRIEF AND TRAUMA

The Body Keeps the Score: Brain, Mind, and Body in the Healing of Trauma by Bessel Van Der Kolk

The Other Side of Sadness: What the New Science of Bereavement Tells Us About Life After Loss by George A. Bonnano

SUDDEN/TRAUMATIC LOSS

Bearing the Unbearable: Love, Loss, and the Heartbreaking Path of Grief by Joanne Cacciatore, PhD

Find the Helpers: What 9/11 and Parkland Taught Me About Recovery, Purpose, and Hope by Fred Guttenberg

The Grief Keeper by Alexandra Villasante (Latinx)

I Wasn't Ready to Say Goodbye: Surviving, Coping and Healing After the Sudden Death of a Loved One by Brooke Noel and Pamela D Blair, PhD

Podcasts

Bereavement Room (featuring representative voices across Black and brown diaspora)

Good Mourning (All things grief with honesty and humor, hosted by two Aussie ladies)

Grief Dreams (hosted by Dr. Joshua Black)

The Grief Gang (a British podcast normalizing grief)

Grief Out Loud (produced by Dougy Center, a national grief center for children and families)

Griefcast (with Cariad Lloyd)

Last Day (a podcast on what's killing us, covering suicide, addiction, and the very tough topics)

Sisters in Loss (focused on pregnancy loss and infertility stories within the Black community)

Terrible, Thanks for Asking (hosted by Nora McInerny)

Support Organizations

Crisis Text Line (Text HOME to #741741)

Compassionate Friends (supporting families after a child dies)

The Dinner Party (virtual and IRL gatherings for twenty- and thirty-somethings)

The Dougy Center for Grieving Children and Families

JED Foundation (suicide prevention and support for teens and young adults)

National Alliance for Grieving Children

Parents of Murdered Children

Seleni Institute Center for Women's Health (support for infertility, miscarriage, stillbirth, infant and child loss)

Tragedy Assistance Program for Survivors (TAPS) (support and programs for those grieving the death of a military loved one)

Resources for Children

MY FAVORITE GRIEF BOOKS FOR KIDS

Ages 3–5

City Dog, Country Frog by Mo Willems

The Goodbye Book by Todd Parr

The Memory Tree by Britta Teckentrup

Ages 4–8

Amos and Boris by William Steig

Badger's Parting Gifts by Susan Varley

Death is Stupid by Anastasia Higginbotham

The Fall of Freddie the Leaf by Leo Buscaglia, PhD

Ida, Always by Caron Levis, MFA, LMSW (Caron also has excellent resources on her website, www.caronlevis.com)

The Invisible String by Patrice Karst and Joanne Lew-Vriethoff

Rabbityness by Jo Empson

When Dinosaurs Die by Laurene Krasny Brown and Marc Brown

Ages 8–12

Each Little Bird That Sings by Deborah Wiles

Love That Dog by Sharon Creech

Tear Soup by Pat Schwiebert and Chuck DeKlyen

YA books

(From "12 Diverse YA Books That Taught Me About Grief," by Alica Forneret, originally published on ModernLoss.com)

All the Bright Places and *Holding Up the Universe* by Jennifer Niven

The Astonishing Color of After by Emily X. R. Pan (AAPI)

Hush by Jacqueline Woodson (BIPOC)

I Am Not Your Perfect Mexican Daughter by Erika L. Sanchez (Latinx)

Long Way Down by Jason Reynolds (BIPOC)

The Sky is Everywhere by Jandy Nelson

The Start of Me and You by Emery Lord

They Both Die at the End by Adam Silvera (Latinx)

We Are the Ants by Shaun David Hutchinson (LGBTQ+)

When We Collided by Emery Lord

Wild Beauty by Anna-Marie McLemore (Latinx)

And also:

Clap When You Land by Elizabeth Acevedo (BIPOC, Latinx, LGBTQ+)

Counting by 7s by Holly Goldberg Sloan

CHILDREN'S SUMMER CAMP PROGRAMS

Camp Erin

Comfort Zone Camps

Experience Camps

Endnotes

Guiding Principle for Using This Book

Horseshoe crab facts. Craig Lesher, "The Horseshoe Crab: World's Most Successful Animal," Nature.org, June 17, 2013. https://blog.nature.org/science/2013/06/17/the-horseshoe-crab-the-worlds-most-successful-animal.

Your Grief Affirmations

No feeling is final. From the poem "Go to the Limits of Your Longing," by Rainer Maria Rilke.

What Is Resilience, Anyway?

Because we as humans have an innate capacity to adapt to loss and function healthily. Donna L. Schuurman and Monique B. Mitchell, *Position Paper: Becoming Grief Informed: A Call to Action*, Dougy Center: The National Grief Center for Children & Families, 2020.

On the flip side, it can also be ignored, and then it may become atrophied. Maria Konnikova, "How People Learn to Become Resilient," *New Yorker*, February 11, 2016, www.newyorker.com/science/maria-konnikova/the-secret-formula-for-resilience.

Trigger Days

Telephone of the Wind. Mari Saito, "Japan's Tsunami Survivors Call Lost Loves on the Phone of the Wind," Reuters, March 4, 2021, www.reuters.com/article/us-japan-fukushima-anniversary-telephone/japans-tsunami-survivors-call-lost-loves-on-the-phone-of-the-wind-idUSKCN2AX03J.

Mizuko Kuyo. Erica Goss, "Mizuko Kuyo, Japan's Powerful Pregnancy Loss Ritual," Modern Loss, October 29, 2017, https://modernloss.com/mizuko-kuyo-japans-powerful-pregnancy-loss-ritual.

Help Is on The Way

Here is a short, creative process altered from a piece that Caron Levis wrote for Modern Loss. Caron Levis, "8 Steps to Writing a Loss Story with Your Child," Modern Loss, February 4, 2019, https://modernloss.com/8-steps-to-writing-a-loss-story-with-your-child.

The Mind/Body Grief Continuum

A note on sleep trackers. K. G. Baron, S. Abbott, N. Jao, N. Manalo, and R. Mullen, "Orthosomnia: Are Some Patients Taking the Quantified Self Too Far?" *Journal of Clinical Sleep Medicine* 13, no. 2 (2017): 351–354.

It's very common to dream of the deceased (human or pet) at least once after a loss. Joshua Black, Kathryn Belicki, and Jessica Emberley-Ralph, "Who Dreams of the Deceased? The Roles of Dream Recall, Grief Intensity, Attachment, and Openness to Experience," *Dreaming* 29, no. 1 (2019): 57–78.

Both the good and bad ones are reflective of your mind processing your grief and trauma while you are asleep. Joshua Black, Kathryn Belicki, Robert Piro, and Hannah Hughes, "Comforting Versus Distressing Dreams of the Deceased: Relations to Grief, Trauma, Attachment, Continuing Bonds, and Post-Dream Reactions," *Omega: Journal of Death and Dying*, February 9, 2020.

Dr. Black found that your dream recall rate is very important for you to "catch" one of these types of dreams. Black, Belicki, and Emberley-Ralph, "Who Dreams of the Deceased?"

Studies have shown that being just half a liter dehydrated can increase your cortisol levels; your heart rate is up and you're breathing more heavily, so you're losing more fluid. Gina Shaw, "Water and Stress Reduction: Sipping Stress Away," WebMd.com, www.webmd.com/diet/features/water-stress-reduction#1.

The butterfly hug was developed by Lucina Artigas during her work with the survivors of Hurricane Pauline in Acapulco, Mexico, in 1998 . . . natural catastrophes. Lucina Artigas and Ignacio Jarero, "The Butterfly Hug Method for Bilateral Stimulation," EMDR Foundation, September 2014, https://emdrfoundation.org/toolkit/butterfly-hug.pdf.

CST involves facilitating or enhancing the body's own natural capacity to heal when trauma or disease processes become overwhelming for the nervous system. "Discover CranioSacral Therapy," Upledger Institute International, www.upledger.com/therapies/index.php.

CST positional therapy for wrists, arms, and hands. Positional therapy for wrists, arms, and hands. Developed by neuromuscular therapist Lee Albert of the Kripalu Center for Yoga & Health, https://kripalu.org/resources/how-relieve-wrist-pain.

They also release feel-good neurotransmitters and pain-reducing hormones that can, at least temporarily, give us reprieve from the immeasurable pain or numbness. Litsa Williams, "Let's Talk About Sex (and Grief)—Part 1," WhatsYourGrief.com, https://whatsyourgrief.com/sex-and-grief-1.

Spending 120 minutes in nature correlates with statistically higher physical and psychological health. Mathew P. White, Ian Alcock, James Grellier et al., "Spending at Least 120Minutes a Week in Nature Is Associated with Good Health and Wellbeing," *Scientific Reports* 9, art. 7730 (June 13, 2019), https://doi.org/10.1038/s41598-019-44097-3.

Living near green spaces in childhood has been shown to be a buffer against mental illness in adulthood. Kristine Engemann, Carsten Bøcker Pedersen, Lars Arge, Constantinos Tsirogiannis, Preben Bo Mortensen, and Jens-Christian Svenning, "Residential Green Space in Childhood Is Associated with Lower Risk of Psychiatric Disorders from Adolescence into Adulthood," *Proceedings of the National Academy of Sciences* 116, no. 11 (March 12, 2019): 5188–5193; www.pnas.org/content/116/11/5188.

Access to window that looks out on green spaces can have a beneficial outcome on surgery recovery and decreased use of pain medication. R. S. Ulrich, "View from a Window May Influence Recovery from Surgery," *Science* 224, no. 4647 (1984): 420–421.

Attention Restoration Theory has shown that looking at green spaces helps us recover from attention fatigue and be more productive. Steven Kaplan, "The Restorative Benefits of Nature: Toward an Integrative Framework," *Journal of Environmental Psychology* 15, no. 3 (September 1995): 169–182.

Their studies show that 39 percent of people felt a decrease in stress simply anticipating humor. Association for Applied and Therapeutic Humor, www.aath.org.

Navigating (And Negotiating) Friendship And Social Dynamics

The guy was kind of awful in major ways—like when he defended slavery and opposed the notion of human equality. Agnes Callard, "Should We Cancel Aristotle?," *New York Times*, July 21, 2020, www.nytimes.com/2020/07/21/opinion/should-we-cancel-aristotle.html.

The 10 People You Meet in Hell, adapted from Erin Donovan, "11 People You Meet in Hell," Modern Loss, October 16, 2017.

In other words, we actually evolved to gossip. Mandy Brownholtz, "Feeling Socially Rusty? Try a Little Light Gossiping," *New York Times*, May 28, 2021, www.nytimes.com/2021/05/28/style/gossip-a-bit.html

Returning to and Getting through Work

Employee orientation would cover more than work safety and sexual harassment—it would also include grief education. Tré Miller Rodriguez, "Game Planning Your Grief: 5 Tips for Returning to Work," Modern Loss, June 19, 2014.

About the Author

REBECCA SOFFER is the cofounder of Modern Loss, which offers encouraging, creative, and keeping-it-real content and community addressing the long arc of grief. She also coauthored the book *Modern Loss: Candid Conversation about Grief. Beginners Welcome.* and is an internationally recognized speaker on loss and resilience. Her work has been widely published with outlets including the *New York Times*, *Glamour*, *Marie Claire*, NBC, CNN, and more. She is a Columbia University Graduate School of Journalism alumna and a former producer for the Peabody Award–winning *The Colbert Report*. Rebecca lives in New York City and the Berkshires in Western Massachusetts with her husband and two children.

@rebeccasoffer | RebeccaSoffer.com

About Modern Loss

Founded in 2013, Modern Loss has become a leader in elevating the conversation around living honestly—and living well—with loss across the long term. Its online magazine has published hundreds of personal essays and practical resource pieces by a diverse range of contributors, its global community gathers both IRL and on its numerous lively virtual platforms, and its popular live storytelling events have featured notable names in comedy, journalism and literature, film and theater, and more.

For more, please visit ModernLoss.com | @modernloss